ALSO EDITED BY MARCUS HARRISON GREEN

———————————

FLY TO THE ASSEMBLIES: *Seattle and the Rise of the Resistance*

978-1-60944-116-6, $15.99

EMERALD REFLECTIONS: *A* South Seattle Emerald *Anthology*

978-1-60944-109-8, $17.00

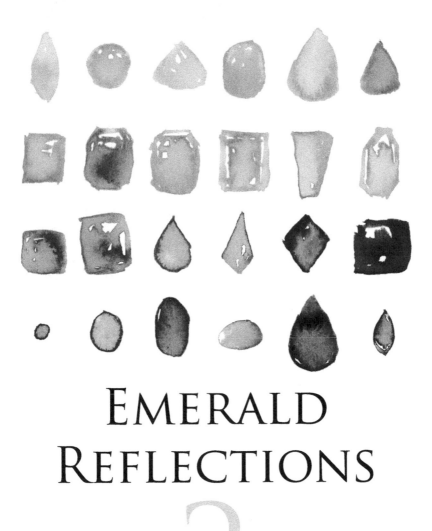

EMERALD REFLECTIONS

A South Seattle Emerald *Anthology*

2

edited by

MARCUS HARRISON GREEN

VERT
VOLTA
PRESS

SOUTH
SEATTLE
EMERALD

Proceeds from the sale of this book go towards supporting
The South Seattle Emerald in continuing its journalistic
mission to serve the South Seattle community and greater Seattle.

Edited by Marcus Harrison Green

Cover art: *©2018 Marisa Manso*

Book and cover design:
Vladimir Verano, VertVolta Design

Published in partnership in the United States by

SOUTH SEATTLE EMERALD
5623 Rainier Avenue South Seattle, WA 98118

& VERTVOLTA PRESS
WWW.VERTVOLTAPRESS.COM

ISBN: 978-1-60944-132-6

southseattleemerald.com

CONTENTS

i INTRODUCTION

POETRY

∿

1 *Not Mine, Oh Really* - Lola E Peters

2 *Dear America* - Nakeya Isabell

4 *Dreaming of Fresh Fields* - Monica Hoang

5 *I See You America* - Alvin "LA" Horn

7 *The Revolutionary Women of South Seattle* - Toshiko Grace Hasegawa

8 *Joseph Bryant* - Namaka Auwae-Dekker

10 *Revolutionary* - Rell Be Free

11 *To the Woman Who Mistook Me for the Bar Staff at My Little Brother's Engagement Party* - Alex Gallo-Brown

12 *In the Land of Subartum* - K. D. Senior

13 *Little Brooklyn (On McClellan)* - Mike Leitner

15 *Little Black Butterfly* - Lee Claiborne

16 *A Cynic's Song* - Kayla Blau

17 *Free Seattle Spring* - Tiffani Jones

18 *Hypocrisy* - Isaac Robinson

19 *In Tune with You* - Alvin "LA" Horn

20 *Exceptionalism* - K. D. Senior

21 *Ebony and Gold* - Harvey Garvey

23 *My Neighborhood* - Alex Gallo-Brown

25 *Passages* - Georgia S. McDade

26 *Memoirs From the Surviving* - Nasra Ali and Namaka Auwae-Dekker

30 *Leveraging the Struggle* - Gabriella Duncan

31 *Our World is Crying* - ChrisTiana ObeySumner

45 *Twisted* - Rae Rose

46 *Thoughts on Luck* - Robin Boland

47 *Worlds Apart* - Kayla Blau

49 *Charleena* - Kiana Davis

52 *Fallen Silent* - Sean Smith

56 *Hunger* - Samira Abbas

57 *Seattle, the Emerald City* - Nikkita Oliver

PERSPECTIVES
ༀ

65 *A Year After the Election,*
    Voting Rights are Still Critical - Hanna Brooks Olsen

70 *Jesus Wouldn't Sweep the Homeless—*
    He Would Help Them, So Should We - Reverend Kelly Dalhman-Oeth

73 *For Latrell Williams* - Marcus Harrison Green

77 *No Place Like Home* - Courtney Weaver

80 *The Scariest thing about* Get Out *is Black Trauma* - Reagan Jackson

84 *Let Them Eat Gravlax* - Lola E Peters

87 *Let's Repeal the Second Amendment*
    So We Can Get On With Addressing Gun Violence - Brian Burgen-Aurand

91 *The Injustice of Jury Duty* - Laura Humpf

94 *What White Marchers Mean for Black Lives Matters* - Marcus Harrison Green

101 *White Americans Are Still Confused About Racism—*
    Here's the Talk We Need to Have - Jon Greenberg

110 *So, What Do We Do With Youth Who Attempt to Kill?*
    - Nikkita Oliver and Gyasi Ross

113 *White Silence Can Be Golden* - Marilee Jolin

117 *Moving Beyond Juvenile "Super-Predator" Rhetoric*
    - Dan Ophardt and Marisa Ordonia

121 *Ending Systemic Racism Can Begin With Seattle* - Marcus Harrison Green

128 *A Billionaire's Burden: Angry Voters and the Making of a Perfect World*
        - Fathi Karshie

133 *Violence in a Non-Violent World* - Ijeoma Oluo

STORIES
〜

143 *One Man's Fight to Free His Son from America's Incarceration Addiction*
        - Marcus Harrison Green

154 *El Centro De La Raza Offers Lessons for Community Land Use*
        - Will Sweger

159 *One Muslim American Veteran Voices her Strength,*
        Despite Uncertain Future - Kelsey Hamlin

162 *Choosing Life: Cancer Support Group Founder Continues to Enlighten,*
        Educate While Battling the Disease - Reagan Jackson

166 *Freedom School Immerses Students in Liberation Education* - Sharayah Lane

169 *Crediting Fitness With Saving His Life, World Champion*
        Power-lifter Uses It to Aid Seniors - Marcus Harrison Green

173 *In Times Like These Poets Have to Poet* - Brian Burgen-Aurand

177 *Homeless Veterans Create Community*
        Together on Beacon Hill - Will Sweger

182 *"The Beachboyz" and Coach Corey Sampson Are the Real Deal*
        - Peter Johnson

186 *To All Good Men: You Must Be Braver* - Danica Bornstein

191 *The Indispensible History and Counter-Narrative* The Journal
        of Ben Uchida: Citizen 13559 *Taught My Son* - Sharon H Chang

195 *An Open Letter to Persons With Guns, Especially Persons Under 25*
        - Georgia S. McDade

198 *A Community Spirit That is Bullet Proof* - Miguel Jimenez

201 ACKNOWLEDGMENTS

203 ABOUT THE EDITOR

Introduction

∽

Shortly after founding the *Emerald*, I was asked if I ever felt like I was simply documenting the death crawl of a community. South Seattle, like the city it resides in, is a victim of swift change. For many, their childhood barbershop, shoe store, and church are either gone entirely, or clinging to existence. Those community lifelines have been replaced by the co-op grocery store, the vegan smoothie shop, or the upscale coffee chain.

The old and new co-exist uneasily. The former awaiting its inevitable defeat to the latter, or so it seems. Those thoughts have often hovered near the peak of my mind during the Emerald's nearly half-decade existence.

But before the fatalism associated with such notions completely grips my will, they're challenged by the resolution that something can only be dead when there is no account of life.

And while many things have been absent during my lifetime spent living in the South Seattle community, tales of life have never been amongst them.

The evidence of that is found in this second volume of poetry, essays, and stories taken directly from the people who vibrantly love, work, and live in what I still believe is this nation's most eclectic domain.

It is that life, lived here, lived now, that continues to be worth the telling. People die not when their heart stops beating, but when their stories no longer have breath.

Stories of this community have invigorated me, along with so many, and will continue to reverberate and endure despite change, or shifts in geography.

Neither will ever be enough to triumph over a narrative of resiliency, ingenuity, resistance, hope, compassion, generosity, and love.

By telling our story, we ensure our community's survival. Along with a life for our community as well told, as it can be lived.

~Marcus Harrison Green

Emerald

Reflections

2

I.

POETRY

Not Mine. Oh Really

by Lola E Peters

That flower didn't birth itself you know
Someone planted the seed
Someone piled on fertilizer
Someone watered it
Someone cleared the ground so roots could spread
Someone did nothing and let the weed thrive
Oh it's your flower, your plant.
You let it grow.

Ignore your racist uncle
Say nothing when a coworker is harassed
Love the food but demean the culture
Sacrifice my security for your safety at the ballot box
Oh yeah? He's yours.

Focus on the flower
while the plant thrives
and ensure more poisonous blooms ahead.
Until you dig into your roots
this will always be
Your orange agent of death
Your murderous flower.

Oh yeah. He's yours.

DEAR AMERICA

by Nakeya Isabell

Dear America,
Land of the free but home of the slaves
I just wanna be free
I don't want the fame
These systems try to way us down
These systems they want to keep us bound
America Dear America

Dear America,
I want you to know all lives matter so yes that includes Black lives too!
And No need to get defensive.
Please listen to hear, And not to speak of your ignorance.
Our mother's, father's and children are crying,
While our corpse hit the pavement
Bang bang, Pop you pulled the trigger again because of your trained fear,
It's these systems
So you ask why Kapernick doesn't reverence your flag
But I ask why don't you admire his response to injustice.
I'm tired of the excuses you use to justify the crime that our very law
    prohibits
Stop allowing your indecisive unpredictable emotions to kill our fellow
    citizens
Impulsive emotion can be destructive
Don't you remember that race was a manmade idea to give power to one
    group and to control others
Can't you see that you are just repeating painful cycles of history that are
    dividing and not uniting us?
What would you like me to tell the youth I serve everyday?

I can't justify your actions as they see themselves, their brothers and sisters
   become your target,

And We want it to stop,

But I wonder if you'll ever choose to listen?

Sincerely,

The People

DREAMING OF FRESH FIELDS

by Monica Hoang

Fresh strawberries and veggies, organic

Meals for my family day and night. But yet

That is just a dream

Open doors to the reality of empty

Calories, empty vitamins, empty proteins,

And empty souls

You wonder why we're sick and what's

Causing it

But you still continued to build more fast

Food places every block, but ask us to eat

Clean?

I See You America

by Alvin "LA" Horn

I'm Black

Woke up Black

If I live to lie down I'll go to sleep Black

When I drive down the street I'll be Black,

And when I sit down for drink and expect good service, I'll be Black

When I go for a job opportunity I'll be Black

When I'm enjoying Black life, and how I have to live, Ill be Black and
conscious of my surroundings

And when I'm pulled over by the police, I'll be super dangerous Black

Even if I live through the encounter, I'll walk away still Black and stunned
one way or another

Here comes the run on sentence like blood running down the street long
and thick:

Sad America … White America what the f*** is wrong with your
consciousness are you so stuck in superiority complexes that the murder
of Black men from people who are trained by your taxes and licensed to
carry a gun and a badge who are only supposed to keep the law, but don't
keep the law they break the law as they kill Black men from babies to the
old… the most innocent

where's your conscience white America why won't you speak up and do-up
change, why do you ignore… I know Black life's don't really matter to you.

Sad America … white America what the f*** is wrong with your
consciousness?

The murder of a Black man from the police who should not be the judge
jury and the hangman or Lyncher

How do you go to sleep?

Got A Black-Eye

Not from a punch … even though we in a fight

And no damn door knob … even though I have seen more damn closed doors and tight asses than a gated community has fake smiles

Got a black-eye

Born with it

Living in America

I see through a Black-Eye

I speak with a Black mind and mouth

I make no excuse to not to conform and accept the status quo

I'm relevant to my period in time

Looking through my Black-Eye

I see you

America

The Revolutionary Women of South Seattle

by Toshiko Grace Hasegawa

We claim space, meet minds, lock eyes, and share stories with each other, revolutionary women.

Writers, organizers, teachers, lawyers, activists or members of the community — we've all had distinct paths but here, in this place, we intersect. What a thing it is to share a timeline in history with all of you, revolutionary women.

I'm a Beacon Hill girl, perpetually. This town is my story and my story is this town. And like South Seattle so many people see my eccentricity as trouble; my multidimensionality as chaos; there's an **emerald** in this rough; it takes one to know one — revolutionary women.

You see like South Seattle, women's stories will go untold. And I commend those who tell stories, or allow their stories to be told, because there is strength and vulnerability in truth;

And in your **totality** multiple truths do exist, and there is nothing that can do **justice** do your divine complexity — Nothing in this world, revolutionary women.

And you might punish yourself for accepting too little, and you will be shamed when society decides you pushed too far.

But when you find yourself weed-wacked, muddy and scratched—well, that's **trailblazing**. Revolutionary women.

Still I believe that only thing in life you truly deserve is yourself. You queens of light. Sun goddesses on high — **Every** day is **your** day. Shine on, Revolutionary women.

We are all a product of what others have done for us, we sit on the strong **hips,** of **S**he who came before. We inherit this legacy from our elders just as we borrow it from the children we may **choose not to** have. But every day I am so honored to share in this, with you. Revolutionary women.

Joseph Bryant

by Namaka Auwae-Dekker

The squash no longer tastes the way I remember

Before white men made a feast

Of my people

The soil was kind

To my aching feet

My mother learned to hold me

From the crisp rhythm

Of the river

Now

The soil does not know who to trust

If the crushing steps upon her

Body

Are those of a

Killers

The river runs red now

So many of us dead

Shot

Last thing we hear is our skin crying open

I will fight

I will lead 4 of the 6 Iroquois nations to fight beside the British

This war has made a corpse of our tribes trust

But I'm doing this so the squash can taste like home again

I do not fight for the British

I fight for my descendants to live peacefully without their culture being
  ripped away

The colonies have pillaged

Want to reap the lands further west

I am a British officer

Fluent in English

A faithful Christian

I command and negotiate and lead to survive

I do not trust the white man

The British promised us land and they gifted it to themselves

I know they do not trust us

Coined us Mohawks, English for man eaters

We are the kanienkehaka meaning people of a place of flint and crystals

I know the white man has already

Carved my tombstone

Joseph Brant born 1743, died 1807

Lived uncivilized

My last words will be

"Have pity on the poor Indians. If you have any influence with the great, endeavor to use it for their good"

don't forget we natives fought

don't forget we were here during the white mans war

My native name is thayendanegea

And i pray that my legacy will not be forgotten

REVOLUTIONARY

by Rell Be Free

Right fist in the sky – Revolutionary
Black Lives, Black Pride – Revolutionary
Love Yourself for Yourself – Revolutionary
Your worth aint your wealth – Revolutionary

I think I'm John Carlos, I think I'm Malcolm X
Reppin on the podium, wonder if I'm next
Cuz I'm goin for the crown or I'm going deaf
If I couldn't do it right then I'm going left
I'm never trippin on this road less paved
pushin past the path comin out unscathed
But everybody got some scars, sum it up to the game
The trauma gave me some bars, I'm getting rid of the chains, huh
I think I'm 2pac with a Pops and a college degree
I think I'm Cassius graduating to Muhammed Ali
If you aint listenin you bouta be a Liston then
Say my name, say my name "Rell Be Free"
Black Lives, Black Pride – Revolutionary
White cops conditioned to think that niggas scary
And Black folx conditioned to think that cops are hate
We got the relevant evidence on the news at 8
I think I'm Kobe Bryant, I'm a volume shooter
I'm a King with a Dream, think I'm Martin Luther
Check the thesis, this the cleanest exegesis
seekin Peace despite the beef until I'm standing next to Jesus
Radical Love, yeah, that's Revolutionary
I get the spirit from inside this fragile heart in my chest
Drippin blood, sweat and tears til there aint nothin left
That's Revolutionary

TO THE WOMAN WHO MISTOOK ME FOR THE BAR STAFF AT MY LITTLE BROTHER'S ENGAGEMENT PARTY

by Alex Gallo-Brown

I, too, mistake myself for a bartender

from time to time.

When I am walking through an art gallery

or private residence, like this one,

I think to myself, that fellow there,

he could use a drink.

Moscow Mule or Irish Car Bomb?

Pinot Noir or Pinot Gris?

It's one of my true talents,

identifying other people's beverage preferences.

I am not a professional—

I am a savant

posing as a layman—

an appreciator of art, say,

or the groom's older brother.

But you, dear woman, saw

saw right through me!

Pasadena woman of the dangling earring

and perfectly coiffed hair,

I met my match in you.

I had thought that I was hidden,

when I was recognizable

by my face.

In the Land of Subartum

by K.D. Senior

A fallow wind falls and the people are ill,
The elders never talked to the snakes,
for the words of men Kill,
but their bodies are laid to waste upon the hill,
they all burn in Subartum!
Long live the King of Subartum!

In a lake of fire they writhe,
while terror tears at the flesh,
and they are burned alive,
mothers and fathers will weep,
even with no tears left to cry,
In the land of Subartum…

Boys and girls scream,
yet the world stands still,
we turn our backs,
while they stack more bodies upon the hill,
the ones that scatter everywhere,
soldiers shoot to kill,
For the king of Subartum…

Rubble marks the graves where they say good-bye,
they say their prayers one last time,
as fire rains down like thunder,
from the sky,
when there is nothing else,
In the land of Subartum…

Desolate Subartum!
Who will bewail thee?

LITTLE BROOKLYN (ON MCCLELLAN)

by Mike Leitner

Rainier Avenue South South Ferdinand
Northwest corner Eastside of Martin
Luther King Junior Way South of South
Alaska sits a space in time and spaces

Little strips of Park Avenue cut Eastern
Madison folks off at the pass above 23rd
Avenue South up on the pedestrian bridge
Where signs hang hung by worker bodies

Doors open easily here to see who's insides
Come out for sale or otherwise given forth
Like vomit next to Lottie's or Panda on walls
Or strings of shoes strung wrapped in wires

Ladies and gentlemen boys and girls alike
Take the train to school and afterschool
Programmed cellphones slipped so coolly
Into tightskin legging or beaded headscarf

Seek truth in Nelson's knowing brush back
Hair that Emanate's spray strokes fence
Have a snobby rooftop moment pulling plug
Lightning signals source unto this garden

Bro in the hoopdy don't mind shit niggas
He playing in a game don't nobody wins
Cold cockin that little Jews joint rockin
Planes overhead home zombie actin dead

Dodger town never knew what they killed
58 or 59 doesn't matter all that cheap beer
Swallowed up in Angie's singing throats
Go ahead and tear them native trees down

Put uppity shut uppity shoot uppity pop
Bottom of the lake Washington bought
Paid in greasy skids washed in dirty jeans
Walk down our southern streets Seattle

Boot all your inherited privileged produce
To the curb lest it rot in rat ridden walls
Kick all your heavenly heroin heavy habits
Lay down brass tacks under diamond needle

STRONG BLACK BUTTERFLY

by Lee Claiborne

She escaped,
but not unscathed;
From a life so severe & cold

But now
Her beautiful smile
Hides many painful stories untold.

Notice the cracks in her wings,
Yet theres no stalling in her flight.

The unhealed bruises on her feet,
Attest to the harshness of past plights.

Though having been pulled
& weighed down, she somehow
Floats gracefully through the sky,

Holding in her spirit
The mystery
Of the strong black butterfly.

A Cynic's Song

by Kayla Blau

I'm asked what I'm hopeful for

What pushes me from the womb of my bed

What keeps me warm and tethered in the storm outside

I shrug in my apathy

my skeptic

my permanent side-eye to a world not yet healed

I scowl at the screeching of headlines and alt facts and every gullible
   headless brute

They're blinking at me expectantly

I'm likely glaring at them accusatorially

Lately my way of hope is just a cynic's song

A bitter remembrance

A necessary salve we spread

Before we can even dream of sleeping

Free Seattle Spring

by Tiffani Jones

The usual, white, fluffy clouds seem harsh and continuous today

An unjust wall blocking out the warm sun

Trying to pluck the love and life out of me in a way

A warning telling me to gather my things and run

There's nothing for me to do

I stand there, paralyzed, and let the white swallow me in too.

The dark is condescending, beckoning me with its shadows

This numbness hurts yet has no feeling

How could I ever leave without feeling shallow

For being so alone, not helping, or willing

There's nothing for me to do

I stand there, paralyzed, and let the black swallow me in too.

The bright rainbows are attacking me

No longer dim or dull

The sudden rush of color is blinding to see

They come at me, raging, like an aggravated bull

There's nothing for me to do

I stand there, paralyzed, and let the colors swallow me in too.

The words try

To bring me back

They take the tears and wipe them dry

Place the smiles that I lack

There's nothing for me to do

I move once again

For the depression has been finally removed

I am free just like you

HYPOCRISY

by Isaac Robinson

Tell me who i am.
The words seeth out of your mouth.
Am i good?
Am i joyful?
Do you know the nights?
The dark?
The times no one is around?
Of course not.

Tell me what to do.
The words contradict themselves.
I cannot be a student and pay for bills.
I cannot figure out what i want to be without failure.
Why must everyone assume i am Perfection,
The very essence of being touched by God.
Maybe no one thinks that.
But your words keep searing into me like
A tiny knife that digs slowly to my heart.

Hypocrisy is a two trick pony with one actual movement.

I have been deceived.
My thoughts echo with the pain of the world.
I think too much.
But,
Who i am, is not who you think i am.
Who, then, am i?

In Tune With You

by Alvin "LA" Horn

I love your B sharp

I like your G minor, even when it has an uncertain groove it makes me sing
low and slow, and hum to your amplification wanting to be your hip-hop
to lift you up when the country and western has you in tears

Your E flat 7th is sometimes erratic in melody, it confuses me, it's not
smooth jazz, it's not Avant-garde jazz that I do better with, but even
then… that long silent space… ah no, I need rhyme, reason and rhythm
to dance

Ah yeah your C major, can make me want to get horizontal and vertical
with you

Although I want to play your F, I know I rock it and remember every
nuance, and we can take it to the bridge and vamp as one, to dance the
dance… but your C clef needs to meet my Bass clef in the middle so we
can orchestrate more effective collaboration

I would love to have to your A augmented 9th walk the blues away

Then I could enjoy the flow of your B sharp 6th's 7th's and 9th's

Then I can play all your notes and funk you to spread out into being in
harmony with my soul

Exceptionalism

by K.D. Senior

We the people,

free the world with democracy,

but bind it with capitalism,

talk of due process,

where money is innocence and poverty is guilt…

While headlines read:

"The world's youngest empire masters Triumph of the Will"

we teach our young to shake hands

with knives behind backs,

cause the first rule of war

is to

–"strike first"

EBONY AND GOLD

by Harvey Garvey

Complete the introduction move to the intellectual
Fundamental prefunk a convo 'tween extraterrestrials
Your levels of carbon give you a special glow
Get tangled in these tentacles I'll never let go

Powered by Kemet comforted by Kush
sliding thru Sudan in a sedan wit an out of town look
Like the Twi from Ghana the Dogon my sponsors
TGA we inscribe Sankofa on our choppers
The forefathers in Morocco, is why they call us Moors 'RiseUp' is the motto

In the word factory making expensive statements
UNITEDSTATESofAFRICA; it's time to run out of patience.
We were given freedom but how we still making payments?
Praying for peace while they're shooting and building space ships.

Kno the basics, in America WE'RE aboriginals
Our history here didn't start as slaves to these criminals
for political purposes they altered our identity
knew that was coming; carved them statues to help our memory.
Hella hieroglyphics all Black to be specific.
You know us when you see us: phenotype too terrific.

The Olmecs we came before Christopher, Columbus
And amongst US is where THEY learned life's literature.
Don't believe me research the EVE GENE…
The Black woman is God makin it look easy, Vickie…..
February '52 a legend was born…
The earth got a jewel that once had the heavens adorned x2…

Vickie Williams: Will I am Victoria…

gave her Life for Enrichment now I am victorious…

She's the oracle, you be Neo, I'm Morpheus…

She was Tubman so that makes us her freed warriors…

She played the background while we were front & center…

Paved a way for an underground railroad of winners…

skin real light but her soul Gold & Ebony…

did Moor for us than Obama and don't you forget it please…

We owe her blood, sweat, tears even oxygen…

She Enriched our Lives and never the opposite…

Her love & legacy resides in that bookstore…

The Great Ancestor to the sky when we look for her…

Vickie

♀♥♀

My Neighborhood

by Alex Gallo-Brown

In my neighborhood
there is no place to sit,
not unless you count the porches
since it is mostly houses here,
but I am tired of my view
of clumped leaves and empty streets,
of women in scrubs smoking,
of men, never more than one but multiple,
dragging firewood from where to where I never ask
although we sometimes wave.
So today I have decided to walk
through the parts of my neighborhood
that I have not gotten to know
simply because I have not bothered to walk
the two blocks in two years
to where the houses butt up against the interstate,
only a thin wall of concrete
separating where the people live
and the people drive,
all those consciousnesses confined to cars
when I have access only to mine—
my neighborhood, my mind.
I pass a pile of plastic shards,
its origin unclear,
a backyard greenhouse
growing who knows what,
a fence of razorwire

dividing houses from a field
of industrial machinery.
On a porch, a man
regards me with indifference and suspicion.
I wave my tea at him and carry on.
On the next block, I sit down
near a sign that says, "STOP."
A small car turns, speeding past me
without a thought.
I realize that I must look foolish
sitting down on the corner
with my mug of ceramic tea,
in search of an indication
of this place warming to me,
or a warning
that I belong.

Passages

by Georgia S. McDade

Separation—from loved ones, from all they knew

first in Africa

then in the "new world"

often repeatedly in the land of the free

psychological pain and suffering then, more later, now, maybe forever

pain transferred to children.

Herded, sold as if they were animals,

bred at the master's discretion

barely enough food for subsistence

shacks, huts for shelter

rags, hand-me-downs for clothes

bodies always at the mercy of earth's elements.

Heavy labor

sun-up-to-sun-down-and-beyond labor.

They must have suffered some of the ailments from which we suffer

and lacked any of the treatment we sometimes get.

Still they survived; some unexplainably thrived.

Lashed and otherwise punished at a whim, they endured

sexual harassment, sexual assault.

The fear must have been overwhelming yet not paralyzing—they moved.

Anyone lifting a voice—not to mention a hand—suffered, sometimes mightily,

suffered death.

We shall overcome.

Yes, no doubt.

But we can say of much we have overcome as we continue to overcome.

Memoirs From the Surviving

by Nasra Ali and Namaka Auwae-Dekker

A conversation between brown brother and light skin sister

Don't come home in a body bag

I tell him

A quiet promise I know he can't always keep

Please come home with most of yourself

I tell him

I cant he says

For this country always finds a way

To butcher brown bodies on the

Sidewalk,

In grocery stores

And county jails

And on channel 7

And on and on and on and on

White people have swallowed us whole

Left no solace or mercy

You can still live in our whips, they say

And offer poison berries as reparations

Tell us to find comfort in the flower beds they have made

Some would call them mass graves

Or the bullet wounds

They gifted us when ship first hit sand

A premature eulogy from light skin sister to brown brother

This promise made gasoline of your body

And a white man's discomfort waiting to lodge itself

Between your ribs

This country sewed a pen to my right hand

Your tombstone to the other

Said "be prepared for when we reap this melanin. Make flames of his body"

You have not died

But every police siren can almost

Carve your name in its steady rhythm

maybe if white men didn't fuck the color out of our people

maybe if trauma didn't make homes in our lungs

Maybe my mother wouldn't be splintered

Beaten by men who learned from their fathers

And their fathers

And the pain that followed the pillage

But white always finds a way into rebirth

Our skin bleached like our streets

We are choking on ghosts

My mother and

Her mother and

Her mother are crawling up my throat

Begging for a home that isn't rusted with brown blood

The hills have eyes where i'm from, refuge is almost impossible to find

Except in the white swan wings of whitified norms

Its chains transcending the tests of time

It wraps around me like a comforting blanket, whispering sweet nothings into my ear

Welcomed by the impressionable mind of a young girl unaware of the history of her pigment

She yearns for the milky skin, for the things awarded to her white peers
For the chains to turn to silk and fall from her form
She yearns for freedom

The hills have eyes where i'm from, this city never sleeps
That is a euphemism for someone who will always be watching

Always there to see, never to help me breathe
They are slowly snubbing out my native tongue like a cigarette
And massaging my roots with chemicals
And chemically lightening my skin
And continuing to tell my people their skin will never win
But they love my melanin
The splash of color i bring to their blank canvas
I am covered in the dust of crushed pearls
Crafted from emeralds and the darkest type of light found
Their teeth ache with rage cause they know this.
They know they need the fruits we produce
They love to fall in love with our flowers without once glancing down at
    our roots.

Split open again and again and again
We learned to mend ourselves
We made a new kind of home
Where the taste of our ache reminded us of a strange fruit
One with a thick skin and impossibly sweet juice
We turned our noose into a ribbon
We got that homemade type of love

That cornbread that ain't soft

Or sweet

Or white washed

We got that I hear god in her voice type gospel

That never miss a beat type soul

That family vibe you wish you could buy

We got it, you can't have it

They took our people with their weapons

We took a knee

They tried to constrict our throats with their systems

That only taught us how to breathe

They wanna keep us under, thinkin they can drown us in the rain

You may have brought us here, but we still the best that ever came.

Leveraging the Struggle

by Gabriella Duncan

restraining the battle
there is a victory
inside the silence
of the wait time
as you exercise
resilience from desire
to commit violence
Even when it is
against yourself
mental fortitude is
no longer valued
if you cloud your
vision by conceding
to the insanity of
egoic nature
the point of
absurdity
peace is built
upon open palms
closed fists are
useless if one
take's the battle
on too soon
fighting a battle
With nothing
but two
bloody stubs.

Our World Is Crying

by ChrisTiana ObeySumner

One:

When I wake up in the morning, and I greet my white husband
When I lay in bed
and wait
for my body to tell me if this is a good day
or a muscle relaxer day
When I remove my cap,
pink and silk
and shake out my kinky curls
When I turn on my bathroom sink
and I immerse my hands
into the water
so hot and soothing.
What a privilege.

When I shift through the pile of shirts
to find the right one
that makes me look
professional
That makes me look
safe
That makes me
fit in

When I pray to God
that I make it home tonight.
When I pray
I don't end up as a story

on the nighttime news.

When I pray

my life

doesn't cascade into nothingness

Like dominoes,

dismantling

tumbling

perfectly

from spark to finish

From a routine stop

to "Hands up, Don't shoot"

to blood pooling on the ground

to "They should've just cooperated"

The genetic expression of my ancestors manifested perfectly in a vessel

holding

a spirit of love

Peace

Empathy

Understanding

Longing

But seen as a melanated dirge

to dominant culture

white culture

who brands me

as Trash

Lazy

Threat

Danger

Animal

Inhuman

All the while,

writing a storied falsehood

about my people

But somehow I make it through because

I "Sure don't act Black."

The path to inclusion

A concept needed

to understand my complexity

My Brown skin

and it's fit in White America

A harsh reminder that

Books and discourse

about identity

is needed to talk

to someone like me

For cultural awareness

For acceptance

For equity

For humanity

An instruction manual for complexity

Complexity beyond the Able-Bodied, Privileged

European immigrants

who somehow became the authority

over the rest of us

Possession is 9/10ths of the law

Unless you have the power

to change

who possesses what

Regardless of pre-existence

A time and culture

of "This is mine now."

Two:

Our Broken World
Long in disrepair
Fighting,
arguing,
accusing,
feuding,
violence,
vitriol,
hate,
hurt
Infection
Spreading
from coast to coast
Like a weeping wound
Running over
into our water,
our oil,
our flora,
our homes
And as the rich, red blood falls
from our body to the floor
So does our humanity flee
from our person
Absorbed
into the universe

The universe

To whom our brothers and sisters

and everyone in between

Prays for harmony

Just to live

without prejudice

Without oppression

Without marginalization

Without discrimination

Just to live

in peace

Our broken world

Buckling

under the weight of our transgressions

Burdened

by the heaviness of our hearts

Lost

in the depth of our sins

Like an abyss

Swirling torrents of torment

persuading our lives

Deeper and deeper

we fall

with ignorance

and hatred

We seek the light

But it cannot shine

Not now.

Not Here

How can we expect illumination

when we've removed all the windows?

We fear difference

but we're already different

We denounce diversity,

but we're already diverse

We abhor change,

but we're constantly changing

We preach scarcity,

but we,

ourselves,

are a scarce and fleeing entity

We defer to laws,

but we're lawless

We reference our morals,

but where is our morality?

Our world cries

It is sick

It is feverish

It shakes and convulses at the action

of it's inhabitants

Perhaps it wonders why

we must destroy it

and ourselves

Perhaps it thinks about ridding itself

of us

Like body lice

Nefarious,

parasitic,

and easily removable

Perhaps the Great Flood was the world bathing

Cleansing itself

of the persistent itching

that accompanies

irritation

and abrasion

Our world is crying

Do you hear it?

Or are you deafened

by the constant chatter of the media

Affirming our division

Discouraging unification

Harmony

Peace

Our world is crying

We soothe ourselves

From the mouths of politicians,

flawed systems,

discriminatory institutions

It'll be OK

It'll be OK

Nevermind

the grieving tears of the world

It'll be OK

Three:

Keep hope ever alive
Because there are those of us
Who've heard the world's plea
Who feel it's strength
buckling under the weight of our actions
Who wishes to bring harmony
and peace
For everyone
Not some
Not part
Everyone
For those old and young
For those sick and healthy
For those poor and rich
Across religion
Across gender
Across race
Regardless of ability
Regardless of fallibility
Regardless of origin

Because there are those of us
Who have been fighting
Who will continue to fight
Who will not rest
until equity becomes equality,

and equality

becomes an ancient endeavor

Because why would we need multicultural competence

in a world who is already competent?

Why would we need cultural awareness

in a world who is already aware?

Why would we need to fight for acceptance

in a world that is already accepting?

Why would we need to demand inclusion when we're already one

Unified

The All Lives Matter folks of the world today would not exist in that world

Because why would we need to remedy

a problem that no longer exists?

Perhaps we may never see this world

in our lifetime

Perhaps our children

will need to continue our fight

Hopefully our grandchildren

only need to deal with our remnants

Hopefully our history books will reflect

on our generation

incredulous of our savagery

Because there are those of us

Who will never stop fighting

until hating someone

for their identity
is a distant,
painful legend
The moral of a cautionary tale
Where children learn about
the damage
we can do
The power
we have
The mistakes
we've made
The time
We've lost
The progression
we've reversed
The peace
we've shunned
Out of nothing
but spite
for our earthly family.

You know,
they say you can't live your life
in a vacuum
But that is precisely
what the world is
A finite foundation,

sealed by a combination of gas

and magnetism,

separating us only by bodies of liquid life

Essentially,

we're roommates

Sharing and living

with the same possibilities for survival

in this vacuum

as the rest of the inhabitants

At least,

in an incredibly optimistic,

theoretical existence

But the possibility exists

for that theory to become reality

And we will continue fighting

And we will continue praying

And we will continue loving

And we will continue educating

And we will continue accepting

And we will continue collaborating

And we will not stop

until there is no more oppression

Until there is no more division

Until the world is soothed

from it's hurt and pain

Because there are those of us
Who know they don't have a choice
anyway
Whether it's due to marginalization
or ethical necessity
Whether they are the target of hatred,
or have an intense hatred
of hatred
Whether they are the hunted,
or those who wish to shield the hunted

We must act
In love and solidarity
We must act
So I'll ask you again
Do you hear the world crying too?

TWISTED

by Rae Rose

His love falls like rain,

Want, a desire born of shame,

With every blow,

I know,

He loves me,

Blinded unable to see,

The love that could be,

If only he would choose me,

The "I love you" he can never say,

Until his temper comes into play,

I love you,

Despite what you put me through,

I love you,

I wish you could love me to,

Broken and bleeding,

Begging, pleading,

Still, I can never reach you,

This love I wanted to teach you,

This cycle that plays again and again,

Trapped in our pain there is no end…

Dedicated to my father whose love was to painful for me to endure.

THOUGHTS ON LUCK

by Robin Boland

I carry around a silver 4 leaf clover in my wallet

Today when I came across it I thought to myself "there's the luck that got you through this year"And then I stopped and thought "Seriously girl? You really think this year was fuckin' LUCKY?"

So what is luck, to me—today?

It's December 1st and it's my last day of chemotherapy

I survived 256 days of a fight with cancer

So am I lucky or am I strong?

Lucky to be strong enough to survive

Lucky to have people to hold me up when I was weak

So, luck looks funny this year but it's here

I can see it now

#WomanPower #StayStrong #KeepFighting

WORLDS APART

by Kayla Blau

Ashley is 12

Latchkey kid, supper in the foil again

Just leave your report card on the bedside table

Soon lost in the piling bills, coffee rings

Court reminders, medications, rolling papers

Her mom say nobody in a shelter should be buying pre-rolls anyway

She say her daughter was a mistake and she let the other one go, go

She say she feels like herself again

Blazes out the door, rollie already lit

She say she'd rather have a normal job but she knows nights and corners
and somebody has to feed the kids

The kids take care of her come sunrise

Tip toe around her, leave her cold eggs before heading to school

Crumpled up homework sinks backpack

Knot in throat grows legs

The kids tell me they have the type stomach ache that doesn't go away

The gnawing type, the knowing type

"I don't know"

Where my mom is who my dad is when we're getting kicked out of here
what school I'll go to next year why my friends parents look at me a little
too hard,

like maybe they know

How to stomach it all

Keep it all together

We're not together

we're not together

Ashley is 12

Summers at the lake house, dinner with the nanny again

Just leave your report card on the kitchen table, soon lost in the piling
Nordstrom bills, medications, to do lists,

Mom say she didn't like how her husband looked at their hired help so she
let her go, go

She say one of their two dishwashers is broken and they're "just trying to
get by"

The kids drink meal replacement shakes come dinner time

She say that flab around the middle is getting embarrassing and somebody
has to monitor what they eat

The kids sit silent in their second dining room,

Sneak moms credit card, hit the mall,

Find solace in the name brands

Come home to self hate & empty rooms

Steal moms liquor, get loaded to mask it

We're not together

We're not together

CHARLEENA

by Kiana Davis

Years ago
I served Charleena Lyles
in my classroom
a room filled with
resilient dreamers
Students just like her
that believed the hope I held in my eyes
for them
the promise for a brighter future....
I taught her
how to study for a test,
how to write an essay,
how to analyze texts,
I taught her what I'd been taught
Respectability and that education would be an equalizer
But I did not teach her
how to stay alive
there is no course for this
I did not teach her
how to bend against inhumanity
to keep her heart beating
inside her black chest.
I did not teach her
how not to be gunned down in her home
in front of her babies
I didn't teach her how to practice
eating the fears of others
To stay alive

but to swallow them
I did not teach her that one day
The spirit of hatred
Would steal everything from her
in order to feed its lust for privilege
I did not teach her
To pray for protection
from oppressive systematic practices
of dehumanization through imprisonment and murder
There is no course for this.
And now we must
Add your name Charleena Lyles
To the growing list of
Hashtagged Say her name pleas
How many more will be added
Until we all stand together and see
 who the real puppeteer is?
We are being murdered in a raging storm
silent throughout America
and the truth behind our deaths will break the back of a nation
that proclaims liberty to for all
but
for all who are not black,
for all who are not brown,
because we fit the description:
The hair on his head was white like wool,
… his arms and feet like burnt brass …

Two years ago, I wrote this poem for Sandra Bland
And now Charlene I will dedicate this poem to you too.
If they kill me,
Because they couldn't handle the truth
Because my loudness uncovered their insecurities
Because the color of my skin is a reminder
of a debt that has yet to be paid
Because I can find beauty in the bottom
of any hell they force me into
and turn the ugliness into coveted gold
Because my womb will birth a generation of warriors
If they kill me
Spread my ashes inside of the wind
Because I will return and I heal the planet.

Fallen Silent

by Sean Smith

*(This poem honors those who have died in King County
this year due to a lack of shelter)*

What makes an indelible impression

Danial Jackson Sodo

Nicole Williams 7900 Aurora N

Kevin W. Bouwkamp MLK Way / E Cherry

What stops you in your tracks

Bruce Sarvis Unknown

Robert Truvino Northgate Library

Hong Ha Unknown

Death stalks the streets

Patrice Pitts 619 3rd Ave

Drew Fife Federal Way

David Chaney 2501 N Northlake Way

Killing the most vulnerable among us

Paul Hitchye JR Federal Way

Paul Duran Aurora Ave N / E John

Lennete Deffley Unknown

Stalking the poor

Mark Rice Franklin Ave E / E Blaine

Kerry Ewing Terminal 30

James McGinnis 8th Ave / Pike

Taking their lives

Ryan Patterson Kent

Michael Barney 130th / Aurora

Michael Draman Kent

If this were a disease

Jennifer Welch Edgar Martinez Way / 4th Ave S

Sean Boarman 4649 Sunnyside N

Anahiah McCarrell 26380 Pac Hwy S

They would call it an epidemic

Armando Brouwer 13050 Aurora N

Kalin Lubben 2101 SW Sunset

Kelly Hall 9th SW/ SW Henderson

You would demand action

Tobias Adams 107th/ Northgate Way

Dianna Newton 226 Aurora

Nicole Popescu Central Library

We would hold our leaders

Dormand McGraw 3rd 1404 3rd

Chester Williams Pac Hwy S / S 240th

Kirstyn Outen Ballard

To coming up with solutions

Heather Rae Vincent Tukwila

Scott Persons 3rd / Union

Carlos Huaman 4th / Pine

But socially we fall mute

Douglas X Smith Tukwila

Dillion Phillip Graham Myers Way/ Hwy 209

Willie B. Tedder I-5 / Dearborn

As they are pushed around

James Ehlinger SW 107th / 15th SW

Steven Carroll Maple Valley QFC

Leighton Dupree 9th/Pike

Swept 601 times

Brett Reyes 9th/PIKE

Robert Lee Latschaw I-5 Overpass / NE 50th

David Dancause Poplar Pl./Bush Pl. S

Their things taken and trashed

Elysha Hayes 7th Ave S / S Snoqualmie

Keith Ice Ayson Highline

Chester Colby 1st/Virginia

Criminalized for their meager existence

Jerald Battee Renton

Kristie Mae Garris Aloha / E Eastlake

Dashaun Griffin 7th NE / NE 50th

All hope and dignity bulldozed under

Anthony James Brown Kent

Tyrone Gathings Linden N / N 137th

John Bethel 2101 N Northlake Way

Amir Budathoki 800 block S Weller

These nameless deaths

Ted Williams 215 W Motor

Anthony Tony Hudson Salmon Bay

Anthony Moss SODO

Of those we knew not

Charles Furman SeaTac

Marc Stokes Lake City

Darrell Williams I-5 Convention Place

Without four walls

Diana Vandecar 9th / Jackson

Stephen Zaragoza Auburn

To shelter and protect them

Jefferson Gordy S Washington / Pioneer Square

Sarah Simmons 102nd/Aurora

Who died alone and have

Robert Joel "Skittles" Brown 50th / 7th NE

Christen Beaty 130th / Lake City Way

(all) **fallen silent**

Hunger

by Samira Abbas

Hunger
Wake up thinking of the day and
How I'll survive, thought what will
We eat today
This hunger stings like a beehive
Days, weeks, months go by
Living off this so called food

Just filled with unnecessary fat
Which slowly deceases your inside
Year's passed you've gained numerous
Body failures and are linked to
Prescription
Their feeding off
Your money
This feeling of despair
Deeper than the shot of a rifle
Man this ain't really fair
Tho this is the poverty cycle

SEATTLE, THE EMERALD CITY

by Nikkita Oliver

The emerald is a stone of love
It soothes and heals the heart
Home is where the heart is
In this city I live somewhere

Between
home and heartbreak
hope and pushout
the haves and have nots

Between
the clouds and weed smoke

Dispensaries replace the brothas on the block
As cranes scrape the sky of her glory
And it all rains down in our faces
The wet will not quench our thirst
Our mouths go dry asking

What story will they tell
When we are all gone
What totem poles will they erect in our places
What streets will they name after our heroes
What colors will they paint the crosswalks
When the city has faded pale
How much will they charge us to visit
Museums telling our stories in voices
We do not recognize
This place anymore

No one wants to leave their home
But especially not without
the promise of return
So we stay
In the shadows of buildings
They won't let us in
But they won't let us go
With the things that we built
Without us
This city is just a place
And not a home

Home of the braves
City named after a Duwamish Suquamish Chief
City built on stolen land
My home an occupied territory
This city a monument to destruction
A homage to genocide
Our home hallowed bones of ancestors
I've never met but I feel shaking
An underground city no longer on fire
But still burning with injustice

And Big Bertha
She will not work today
Will not gnaw at the bit
Will not penetrate sacred land
This drill will not leave us
A viaduct to freedom

She will not make meal of our medicines
And pretend it does not hurt
To sale off our bodies
On the auction block of industry
In the name of progress

How do you build a free way to liberation
On the backs of people
Too occupied with survival
When we can barely pay rent?

How do you reclaim a place
That was never yours to begin with

How do you wrap your ill-fitting mouth
Around a name you cannot say
Without changing it?

How do you tell a story
So honest, so authentic
The truth is undeniable
And the lie has no place left to hide
And you, even you, are
Transformed for the better?

How do I tell a story
In this city where I live somewhere
Between
victim and villain
occupied and colonizer
pushed out and gentrifier?

This city was once a rainforest

Growing greener everyday

Now we blow trees just to forget

The feeling of being unwanted

Of being uprooted and rarely replanted

So we never grow

as green should as we could

Emerald

first translated from Sanskrit

"Marakata"

meaning "the green of growing things"

And this city is growing greener

Everyday in the wrong way

And I can only think of one way

To change it for the better

To tell our stories

To let them fall

A waterfall of tears

On a people too dry to see their own ash

To tell our stories

To never give up or give in

To the silence threatening

To quiet our existence

To tell our stories

We will not make one dimensional relics

Of three dimensional beings

We cannot afford to lose ourselves
Our stories make us what we are

The world is not made of atoms
It is made of stories
A city is not made of buildings
It is made of people
People are made of stories
We build ourselves out of
Disappearing
Is a story we will not be

Home

Is where the heart is
And my heart is here
In the Emerald city
Somewhere between
Home and heartbreak
Is a gem–an emerald
Meant for so much more
Than some oligarchs crown

The Emerald is a stone of love
It soothes and heals the heart

What the mind forgets
The heart will not
And this city is forgetting
It will only grow as big as our hearts

And our hearts will only grow
as big as our stories

So let's tell the best story we can tell
Our home,
Our hearts depend on it

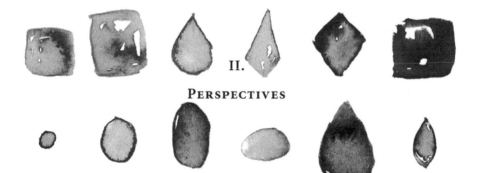

II.

PERSPECTIVES

A Year After the Election, Voting Rights Are Still Critical

By Hanna Brooks Olsen

Nearly a year has passed since the surprising events that unfolded on November 9, 2016. As such, many voters who, last winter, were passionate and vocal about the need to reform the system have moved from talk of Hamilton electors to current-day damage control.

With the Presidential results long since finalized and every last-ditch effort exhausted, Puerto Rico, access to high-capacity firearms, and children's healthcare have taken center stage. Even impeachment seems unlikely.

The narrative is somewhat resolved—Hillary Clinton was a failed candidate, the liberal media overlooked the real numbers of angry whites, and the Republican Party would do anything it could to secure a win. Russian meddling seems nearly a foregone conclusion—though few people seem willing to actually make much of it.

Last year's election was not the first time that the voting system failed millions, whether through the electoral college—where the winning candidate received many fewer votes—or through massive disenfranchisement. For many voters, the chatter preceding Inauguration Day sounded an awful lot like that which followed the election of President George W. Bush, complete with mental images of hanging chads and rigged machines.

And, much as it was in 2004, most talk of revamping the electoral college ebbed away when the reality of the new administration set in, only to be dusted off again the next time that a President is chosen not through the number of ballots cast, but through a somewhat arbitrary and antiquated system where some votes simply matter more than others.

Which might lead a person to wonder: How will the 2016 election impact future races, if at all? And how can Washington be a leader in voting rights, access, or even a massive overhaul, if it at all?

Us vs Them

For all intents, Washingtonians have it pretty good for voting. We don't need to stand in line, we don't need to vote on a specific day, and we don't need to worry about our votes being hacked.

Primarily, this is due to the resources our state and local governments have poured into security and access. King County Elections is widely recognized as one of the most meticulous and forward-thinking elections office in the country. And while the department certainly has issues—like historic access gaps in South Seattle—they've been working on it, adding ballot boxes and new efforts to reach voters. In April of this year, they launched a large grant with the Seattle Foundation for the express purpose of voter outreach in underserved areas.

Of course, Washington still has plenty of problems left to work out; paper ballots get lost and distributing information about how to replace them is difficult. As the Seattle area becomes a destination for more and more immigrant and refugee communities, the need for additional language services has become a greater issue. The requirement for stamps is also not ideal—though Senator Bob Hasegawa has introduced a postage-paid proposal and King County Elections has been experimenting with small counties for almost a year.

Washington has also held out against at least one Federal program—the REAL ID law—which requires additional steps.

To obtain a driver's license in Washington State, a person needs some proof of who they are, but not any proof of citizenship. Previously, this has allowed residents who may be undocumented (which can include those born outside of the country, those who may have misplaced or never had access to their birth certificate, or those who can't afford to replace those documents) obtain some forms of documentation and avoid additional punitive measures, like being ticketed for driving without a license.

It has also meant that they could potentially register to vote—one of the reasons that automatic voter registration has presented a bit of a complex problem. If voting requires a driver's license and a driver's license requires proof of citizenship, it could be more difficult, not less, to vote for some.

Secretary of State Kim Wyman has emphasized her support of the REAL ID law—she's the only top-level elected official who identifies as a Republican in Washington State—the Governor has shown little will to speed up compliance. At present, residents of Washington are in a "grace period."

Other states, though, are cracking down even harder.

Poll taxes in Alabama, voter ID laws in Texas, and any number of smaller, more subtle methods of deterring voters have made all the more difficult to get out the vote in time for the 2018 midterms—by design.

For all the lefties who threw up their hands because Clinton just wasn't good enough, there are pieces of evidence that it was voter suppression which cost her the Oval, not a lack of interest or passion. Voter ID laws kept as many as 17,000 Wisconsin residents from two counties from voting in 2016; she lost the state by less than 1%.

"Black voters and poorer voters more heavily supported Clinton; they were also more heavily affected by the voter ID law," reports the Washington Post.

Voter ID laws aren't the only way that People of Color are kept from voting—long lines, inclement weather, lack of access to transportation, reduced voting locations, and the fact that in many areas, the middle of the day on a Tuesday is the only time to vote all contribute. And they're all ways that Washington has worked to make voting easier.

However, there is no silver bullet—and Washington can't lead if the rest of the nation doesn't follow, or even agree that there's anything wrong. Because in addition to the myriad problems with the current voting system, there is also the macro issue of the system itself.

ADDRESSING THE ELECTORAL COLLEGE

There has been no shortage of ink spilled over the electoral college, a system which turned 140 years old in February. Designed to ensure that candidates couldn't win simply by campaigning to cities and other dense areas, it divides the nation up not by votes, but by regions.

Harvard Law professor Lawrence Lessig has been campaigning to reform it. Fear of a party schism has Republicans like John Kasich wondering about it. Clinton told CNN that it was time to abolish it.

This is a tall order, though; a two-thirds majority is required to ratify the Constitution and, at a time when Republicans can't even get the votes to repeal and replace the Affordable Care Act, it's unlikely that that many lawmakers could agree to fundamentally change the way voting is done.

Robert Reich has another idea—he's lobbying for states to work to nullify the electoral college.

"All that's needed in order to make the Electoral College irrelevant is for states with a total of at least 270 electors to agree to award all their electoral votes to the presidential candidate who wins the popular vote," he explains. Currently, states totaling 165 electoral votes already do this—including Washington.

Which means that states totaling 105 electorate votes need to pass similar laws. Unfortunately for the movement, most of the states that already do it are those which tend to be more sympathetic to voting rights and access in general—states like New York and California. And, almost a year after the election, those states, too, have their hands full—if they're not trying to flip Congressional seats, they're trying to batten down the hatches against regulatory repeals that end in flooding, forest fires, or or worse.

WHERE WE ARE NOW

It seems unlikely that a massive eschewing of the electoral college is in the future of the country, regardless of how many pithy videos are released by thought leaders—if only because it has become such a chore to conduct even the most basic of governance. We can't get clear water to Puerto Rico—how are we going to massively overhaul the voting system?

Voting is, in and of itself, extremely politicized; historically, it has been a way for white people, for men, and for landowners to maintain control and dominance. The ability to vote has been held over those trying to attain some semblance of participation. In the modern era, when the laws so clearly state that voting is, indeed, for everyone, there is a greater element of sneakiness.

Progressives view more access to be a definitively good thing, while conservatives have used the (unproven, unscientific, unfounded) spectre of "fraud" to galvanize their constituents. As a result, voting, like so many other things, is a place to stump and argue, rather than work collectively.

What fraud there has been, it seems, has benefited the right, though.

This has spurred activists toward the nuclear options—abolish the electoral college, move to ranked-choice voting, abandon the secret ballot in favor of even greater convenience.

And some of this may be achievable on a local level; King County Elections heard the call for more ballot boxes in the south end and the number of ballot boxes was increased. New languages are being added to voter's guides every year. REAL ID is still not in full effect, leaving space for people to get registered to vote even without expensive and often inaccessible paperwork.

In another year or so, the next Presidential election cycle will begin heating up once more—and it'll be interesting to see if the electoral college is again on the agenda for discussion.

Jesus Wouldn't Sweep the Homeless— He Would Help Them, So Should We

by Reverend Kelly Dahlman-Oeth

Every morning when I get to church, I say, "Good morning" to Danny and Trevor who are asleep on the concrete courtyard. They are always eager to see me and grateful that I am there to invite them in to get warm.

The other day I found Jennifer's clothes and HIV medications in the bushes at church, and I brought them inside to keep them safe. I don't know her, but I consider myself her pastor.

Every time he's released, Chris shows up to sleep on the porch until he loses the battle with the mental illness that make his behavior unacceptable to others.

A few years ago, I conducted Debi's memorial service after she died in her car in the Safe Parking program at the church.

Even though I'm a United Methodist pastor, and not a Catholic priest, Gil always teased me, and called me "Father." I still grieve for my gentle friend knowing that he died while he was living in a tent.

Yes, I am a pastor. I am educated, employed, housed and I have good healthcare. As an accident of birth, I am also a white, straight, U.S. born, cis male. The sum total of those characteristics put me at the top of the food chain when it comes to power and privilege in this country.

As a pastor, I am appointed to Ronald United Methodist Church in Shoreline, a church that sold property in a partnership with Hopelink and Compass Housing to recently open a 12,500 square foot food bank and service center and 60 low-income housing units.

As a pastor, I have something in common with our elected officials and all those who are paid to serve and protect. Specifically, we are all responsible to serve all the people in our community: rich and poor, Republican and Democrat, housed and unhoused.

As a Christian, I strive to follow the life and teachings of a first-century Middle Eastern penniless, homeless rabbi that I know as Jesus Christ. This Jesus spent three years healing the sick, feeding the hungry, and telling the poor that they are God's beloved children worthy of dignity and respect.

Jesus also had plenty to say to those of us with power and privilege, significantly, "those to whom much is given, much shall be required."

So, I spend a great deal of my time with those who live on the margins of our society. Indeed, I do not understand what it means to be a Christian if I am not among those with whom Jesus would have spent most of his time: the poor who live on the street; the addicted who battle the demons of drugs or alcohol; the hungry and lonely who come to eat at our free community dinner each week.

Gil and Debi were my siblings. Jennifer and Chris are God's beloved children. Danny and Trevor are not trash to be swept away because corporations or wealthy homeowners have influence over elected officials.

Their lives are just important as the millionaire tech employee and the elected officials. They are sacred.

They are my responsibility, and they are your responsibility, and frankly, they deserve better from me, from us, and from our elected officials.

Sweeps do not solve homelessness. They are inhumane and abusive and expensive.

No one starts doing drugs because there is now a safe injection site in their neighborhood. Clean injection sites do not lead to drug use, they make it safe for those who are possessed by the demons of addiction, and they make it safe for the larger community.

Many of us will continue to learn what we can do to provide safe, caring places for those struggling with mental health issues, but we are no substitute for the trained professionals who are overwhelmed and underfunded.

The HOMES tax can make a big difference in funding housing and vital services for people like Danny, Trevor, Jennifer, Chris, Debbie, Gil, and so many others. Taxing the biggest, most prosperous corporations in our city to fund these services is carrying out Jesus' injunction, "those to whom much is given, much shall be required."

I firmly believe that budgets are moral documents. Municipal, county, state and federal budgets that favor corporations and the rich, while they ignore those who live on the margins are immoral.

I will continue to love and serve my vulnerable siblings, and I implore you to join me, whether you are part of a faith community or not; whether you are an elected official or part of a corporation that benefits from our tax dollars; whether you are one of the wealthiest among us or an average voting citizen like me.

FOR LATRELL WILLIAMS

by Marcus Harrison Green

Childhood officially ends the moment you learn your friend was murdered.

Before then, regardless of how many years spent bumbling around on this spinning rock, there still exists a faith in the resiliency of tomorrows.

Your heart still clutches tightly to the adolescent conviction that tomorrow's arrival carries with it hope, and luminous possibilities to vanquish whatever darkness engulfs your today.

But that belief evaporates once you hear the person you roamed high school hallways with, the person who helped an awkward loner endure a terrible high school experience, the person who helped you persist in your seemingly delusional passion for writing, died before his time, killed just a mile from your home.

I found out recently that my high school classmate Latrell Willams was identified as the victim in the fatal shooting that took place Tuesday night near the Lakeridge neighborhood. According to police reports, Latrell died after suffering multiple gunshot wounds. No one yet knows exactly what happened, or why, as the case is still ongoing.

Latrell's fatal shooting was one of three to take place in South King County in a week's span—receiving scant attention from our political leadership.

Speculation coming from local television stations, neighborhood social media groups, and Next Door haven alike, followed the typical script re-enacted whenever a black male is killed in a shooting in the South End. It must be a gang thing, the victim himself was probably a gangbanger, a thug, or a homeless person in a dispute over drugs. The usual monikers are painted on an unknown murdered black man, his life now a blank canvas colored in by an ignorant perception.

Initially, I gave only a passing thought about the shooting, caught up in the frenzy of a news cycle continuously vomiting up one dismal tale after the next.

My shame came from recognizing that I too had originally dismissed—just another sad tragedy, a story that happens to often—because I, like the others had casually reduced the life of who I thought was an unknown person, to a stereotype.

And, while I can't speak to every aspect of his life, I can testify to those I knew. Latrell was anything but stereotypical.

My mind raced back to our high school days. Like me, Latrell was a black South Seattle bred student exported to a predominantly white, affluent school. Unlike me, he had hit the genetic jackpot. As the star running back our senior year, his muscles seemed constantly pregnant, about to give birth to another. Black Hercules, the "L-Train", Latrell looked like the love child of granite and titanium.

Despite his talent for athletics, we aligned because we were still two people who never wholly seemed to fit in, unable to completely give away all of ourselves to an atmosphere that rejected a large chuck of our personas.

Each year I did my best to exhaust every absence I could from a school I dreaded attending each morning. I counted down every minute until the clock hit 2:30pm, bringing the sweet salvation of the dismissal bell, and the reprieve it brought from the shame of being black and poor.

But Latrell made my captivity there bearable. The star running back would sit at the cafeteria table with me, right at the exact moment I began thinking I had been placed in contagion because no one dared come within a 10-foot radius.

Naturally laconic, every word he spoke had purpose. He used them to convince a 120lbs rail thin 5-foot nothing senior to join the football team in during my final year of high school—as much as I hate to admit it the best experience of my high school years.

It was how he persuaded me to continue showing up to class after I had been warned that one more absence would result in me automatically failing the year. I had the bright idea to simply stop showing up to school so my parents would be forced, or so I thought, to let me finish out high school at Rainier Beach.

It was how he got me out of trouble all those times I was busy doing every single one of those lurid things teenagers swear up and down to their parents they're not doing, but of course are.

 It was how he persuaded me to finally enjoy a little bit of my experience at a high school I spent three and a half years hating with the raw intensity of a thousand white hot suns.

He rarely smiled, as he seemed to always be navigating his place in the school, and the world, along with his future's course as a football recruit, but still fixed in my mind is the one he laid on our graduating class as he was named the athlete of the year. Though he was looking out at all of us, I kept thinking it was directed at me, saying, in his typical understated way, "We South End boys made it."

Our paths diverged after high school, he went off to play football at Montana State, and I went California Dreaming in Los Angeles.

They converged again though, when I returned to Seattle, giving up one fantasy to pursue another.

I began bumping into him almost every day at the Rainier Beach library.

It was the only office space I could afford in the early days of the *Emerald*. He would be there just as religiously working on scripts for a show he had in mind to produce one day, our friendship was rekindled. We talked about our shared love of storytelling, contrasting our chosen mediums. His love for the visual was matched by mine for the written word.

For that, he had my kinship, but he had my respect for the fight he was undertaking.

He shared with me his long, protracted custody battle over his son that had lasted more than year. The child had been suffering noticeably in a toxic situation. I remember thinking then, the same thoughts as today: in a world where black men are constantly maligned for being absentee fathers to the detriment of their families, here was a determined Latrell obsessed with reuniting with his 12-year-old son, no matter the cost in money or time.

He would keep me regularly updated on the progress, or lack thereof, and we'd encourage each other to show up every day to chip away at our dreams. We struggled, strived and survived in those early days when our dreams seemed to be unable to escape irrelevance, and failure seems inevitable.

But his words lifted my spirit as they had a decade earlier, telling me whether "sprinting, walking, or crawling—just keep moving forward, Marcus."

Months of Sundays have passed since we saw each other last. Childhood really is gone, and with it a reliance on tomorrow's grace to speak words foolishly delayed.

He never waited to speak the one's I needed to hear. I wish I hadn't reserved my own in thanking him for feeding a scrawny kid belief who previously feasted on a steady diet of doubt. I wish I had capitalized on our shared present to express gratitude for steering a reckless teenager's destiny away from the treacherous hazards along life's turnpike. I wish I would've said I love you, Latrell.

But as you once told me, it's never too late to do what needs doing.

No Place Like Home

by Courtney Weaver

This past week, yet another homeless encampment was gutted by the city of Seattle. I can't help but think how a slight change in my own circumstances would leave me out in the cold. You can't talk about the homeless crisis in Seattle without talking about domestic violence. Domestic violence is the number one cause of homelessness. People ask me way too often, "Why didn't you leave?" Well, actually mostly because of financial reasons.

People—myself included—often talk about the worst part of the relationship, the abuse, when discussing intimate partner violence, but neglect to mention that the violent parts account for a very small percentage of the relationship. Over my past five years of violence research and policy advocacy tracking hundreds of shootings and fatalities, I've learned that domestic violence thrives on extremes; While the bad times are absolutely terrible, a victim's perception is often muddied by the good times—which, in contrast, can be very, very good.

Seattle has the ninth most-expensive cost of living in the world. Affordable housing is difficult even in an ideal healthy relationship. If a relationship is a roadmap of decisions, sometimes you have to make bad decisions just to keep a roof over your head. Financial control is one of the most pervasive and insidious forms of domestic violence and is not something that happens overnight. It is a slow game of power-and-control dynamics that normalize the violence that is precluded by the honeymoon phase.

Often this normalcy and adaptation shifts the dynamic of the relationships so subtly that by the time you realize what is occurring, the reality of making a clean break from this person while maintaining your financial obligations is unrealistic. Not to mention jarring to uproot your life to that extent to start over.

The financial impact of domestic violence is far-reaching and can be devastating for years to come. I lived in a domestic violence shelter for three months in 2011 after I moved back to Seattle for medical treatment, ultimately tallying 14 reconstructive surgeries in two years. On January 15, 2010 my abusive boyfriend Kenneth Fiaui shot me in the face and arm in a botched murder-suicide.

He was sentenced to 10.6 years and will be released from prison on May 31, 2019 with no parole and no violent felony conviction due to the terms of the plea bargain. Arnold Schwarzenegger had cut all domestic violence funding a mere four months before I was shot. At that time, my hometown of Seattle had many more resources to help get me back on my feet.

Again and again, I've seen that distancing and "it couldn't have been prevented" rhetoric is a common reaction to domestic violence tragedies. On Oct. 30, 2015, Honorario Yango shot and killed his daughter Carmen Dela Isla and her daughter Anahila Cowherd in a double murder-suicide. Anahlia Cowherd was a bright and precocious student at Aki Kurose middle school.

As is often the case, the signs of abuse were well-documented in the months preceding the shooting.

Carmen Dela Isla had moved back to live with her father five years prior to the shooting because of domestic violence—she had taken out a protection order against the father of her child, citing physical abuse. I assume that was not a decision Dela Isla wanted to make, but that she was making the best choice she could with the limited options and resources available to her.

Financial abuse is the number one reason people stay in abusive relationships and occurs in 98 percent of all abusive relationships. On the night of October 30, 2014—four days after the Marysville-Pilchuck High School shooting—Dela Isla confronted her father and threatened to call the authorities. Eleven-year-old Anahila had chronicled the ongoing sexual abuse at the hands of her grandfather for 15 months in her now-defunct Wattpad diary, declaring I'm Anahila Cowherd, 11 years old, 5th grade, and I'm gonna bring justice to all girls who have been touched."

Dela Isla's 10-year-old son was present at the time of the shooting. He escaped through a shattered window and was found walking down the street, barefoot with bloody feet. Local news outlets at the time reported that the child was "unharmed" by the incident. *He's not dead, so he must be fine, right?*

Mayor Ed Murray arrived at the scene in a frenzy and held an impromptu press conference.

"One thing I would say is the neighborhood itself is safe" Murray added.

To paraphrase, the message of the press conference seemed to be *It's okay! It's not a threat to the community, it's just domestic violence.* Ignoring the fact that 57% of all mass shootings in the United Sates are domestic violence.

The cognitive dissonance surrounding these two overlapping issues is deafening. As someone who works in policy, Mayor Murray should know that, statistically, domestic violence is a threat to the community. Murray himself is a survivor of domestic violence—he even featured survivors of domestic violence in one of his campaign ads against Mayor McGinn, falsely claiming that domestic violence rose by 19 percent while McGinn was in office.

The rise in domestic violence fatalities over the past few years is not surprising considering the severity of our homelessness crisis. It is, however, preventable. Access to affordable housing and domestic violence services are two of the most influential ways our city can provide safety and stability for the entire community.

THE SCARIEST THING ABOUT *GET OUT* IS BLACK TRAUMA

by Reagan Jackson

I hate horror movies. They linger. Long after the screen goes black I am reliving every cringe-worthy moment. So when I saw the preview for *Get Out*, I was like, wait: Is this a horror movie or is this racism? Is this a horror movie about racism? Oh hell no. I definitely don't want to see that.

Eventually, I succumbed to curiosity and peer pressure. True to the genre, *Get Out* is a movie that lingers, but in a very different way than most. It's the subtle violence that gets under your skin. Writer and director Jordan Peele does a masterful job of creating scene after scene filled with micro-aggressions, white privilege run amok, and downright awkward racist interactions.

The movie begins with Rose (Allison Williams) and Chris (Daniel Kaluuya) making googly eyes at one another, establishing themselves as a couple in love. All the black women sitting in my row (myself included) gave a collective eye roll.

Becky meets a Brother. Okay. That's only the plot of like 900 other movies (#savethelastdance #guesswhosecomingtodinner #Othello). And Rose is the quintessential Becky, perky and progressive, the daughter of parents who would have "voted for Obama a third time" if they could.

They discuss their plans for Chris to meet Rose's family. Chris asks if they know he's black. Rose says no, because she is entirely too post-racial to have really noticed that he is black, let alone mentioned that to her equally post-racial family. She also lets it slip that he is the first black man she's ever dated (yeah right) which so perfectly frames the paradox of white people wanting to be both color-blind and congratulated on their sophisticated race relations at the same time.

Chris calls his friend Rod (played by comedian Lil Rel Howry) who tells him pretty much everything everyone in the audience is thinking. *Don't go.*

This is a bad idea. Something isn't right!

But of course, Chris goes anyway, because white people inviting you to white spaces with other white people that may or may not be cool is actually an everyday kind of thing. What follows is a montage of way too true shit that happens when you are black in white spaces, beginning with a slightly new twist on an old classic, the D.W.B. (Driving While Black).

While on the way to the countryside, they hit a deer. It's jarring. They are both stunned. When the police officer arrives, though Rose was the one actually driving, he asks to see Chris' driver's license. One of them is stunned by this. One of them is not. You can guess who.

So Rose pulls out her white feminist crusader cape. After a short and snarky assertion of her white privilege, they are back in the car and on their way. Here you see that first crack in the lovey dovey "we are a couple" façade. It's that moment where two people realize they were raised differently and have completely different understandings of what just happened and why.

Read: that moment when Chris remembers that Rose's whiteness can be dangerous (#EmmitTill) and Rose realizes for .5 seconds that the post-racial bubble she likes to live in might not have room enough for two.

Throughout the movie we watch Chris rationalize his relationship, again and again, bestowing unsolicited silent forgiveness for all this bullshit simply being with Rose requires of him, and all the lies and mental gymnastics it takes to keep believing "it's not that bad." Except it is that bad.

When they get to the house, Chris can't wait to call Rod. This is a thing. When that crazy and or crazy making racist thing happens, no matter how cool your white friend, colleague or partner is, you have to call your black friends or family members to debrief because they actually understand how you feel and can make you laugh about it. Unsurprisingly, the humor in this movie is a big part of what makes it work. It's what kept me watching as the storyline drew us into worst-case scenario after worst-case scenario.

I promise not to drop any more spoilers. Everything you previously read takes place in the first 15 minutes of the movie. And come on it's a horror movie, so you kind of know what's coming, twists and turns, bloodshed, and general scariness. But I will say this, it was funny, it was scary, it was honest, and now I can't stop thinking about it.

As I left the theater I was inundated with memories of my first boyfriend, a white boy from Two Rivers Wisconsin that I met at church camp. He came to Madison to take me to my homecoming dance, so when he invited me to be his date to his school formal, I begged my parents to let me go.

Lengthy conversations ensued. *You want to go where? With who? Stay where? Really?* My parents were very hesitant to let me go and told me flat-out that they didn't think I would have a good experience, but true to their parenting style they decided that they would let me make my own mistake, but not without support. My dad drove me to Two Rivers. He met the boy and his parents (gave the boy the stare down that black fathers are famous for) and then left me there to endure one of the most awkward and humiliating experiences I have ever had.

There were times during the movie where I wondered if Jordan Peele had secretly followed me around Two Rivers to write down the things white kids and their parents said to me. Then I realized, no, this is actually a universal black American experience, but one that for the most part goes unsaid.

We watch documentaries about slavery or the civil rights movement. Racism is depicted as fire hoses and dogs, confederate flags and white sheets, all open and obvious. It's rare to watch a movie that openly addresses the intimate injustices, the small ways in which your white friends fail you, not by saying the fucked up thing themselves, but by putting you in a situation where that trauma can and does occur. Sometimes it happens so quickly or it's so subtle that they don't even notice. You go home feeling terrible and needing to process and for them it's like it never even happened. This movie lives at the intersection of this disconnect. It takes a long festering wound and picks at the scab until you're left bleeding and raw.

Get Out puts white people on blast in an intense and at times entertaining way, but it also spills the tea on black folks. We have been enduring racial trauma for so long that we have normalized it to a certain extent, learned to laugh about it, learned to side eye, suck it up and drink about it. It's a survival tactic. But what happens when you just can't anymore? What happens when your worst fears are realized and there is no turning back? When you can't keep pretending over and over again that whiteness isn't a psychopathic disease systematically trying to silence, dominate, infect, subdue, and kill you?

Chris shows so much compassion. You can tell he really wants to make it work. He wants to believe that his girlfriend is genuinely a good person. He wants to believe that he just has to endure the unpleasantness and that this will just be a fucked up story to laugh about at the bar. But whiteness is coming for him and the choice is clear: stay and submit, or stand up and get out.

LET THEM EAT GRAVLAX

by Lola E Peters

The most difficult part of writing this is deciding where to focus my anger: the tone-deaf billionaires, and their minions, who are thoughtlessly tearing the fabric of our community, the "news" media that pass off press releases as reporting, or our public officials, who say the right things and then do the exact opposite. Together they create a false narrative that is eroding much of the beauty of our region.

In 2012, performance artist C. Davida Ingram created *Detour*, a cell-phone tour of Seattle's Cascade neighborhood. The title was a reference to the many roadways being redesigned to accommodate the neighborhood's changes. She used key locations in the area to tell the story of transition and displacement that was driving away long-time, blue-collar, mostly white residents out of their single-family homes and replacing them with multi-story office buildings and condominiums. She raised questions about the human cost of dismantling stable community relationships and institutions. She asked whether our town's values incorporated the sustainability of human life as part of the environmental conversation. She invited us to clarify our priorities and vision for the future.

Never heard of the Cascade neighborhood? Oh, it still exists, but you probably know it as South Lake Union, or, if you're given to snarkiness, Amazonia or Vulcanalia North. It has been rebranded to match its shiny new look and feel. Thanks to Paul Allen's property-gobbling monster, Vulcan, single-family houses and small businesses have been replaced by bio-tech laboratories and high-tech code factories. It's now the battleground between decades-long houseboat residents and new hillside denizens who want them gone because they clutter their view; between retired homeowners and the ever-growing property taxes pushing them out; between the Seattle Department of Transportation and the rest of us.

Have you read all the articles in the *Seattle Times* about this displacement? How about from our supposedly grassroots, mainstream, regional, online media? Anyone? Anyone? Bueller? Has any local media followed stories of the families who were pushed out of Cascade?

There used to be a thriving arts community there, what media has reported on where the artists went?

But I bet you've read about the cool thing Amazon is doing: providing housing for low-income families. As proof that the company has a heart, it is kindly loaning an old motel it owns, and plans to tear down in a year, to Mary's Place, a non-profit that provides transitional housing for homeless families. Articles in both the *Times* and *Crosscut.com* all but pant at the generous social responsibility being displayed by our region's mega-employer. We are apparently supposed to forget how those families became homeless and how the neighborhood became unaffordable. Oh, and let's also not notice that this generosity lasts for one year. ONE YEAR. Then Amazon will apparently ask Mary's Place to move their operation to another vacant property while they plant yet another skyrise where the motel currently sits. Yay. Yay?

Across town, Paul Allen, father of property monster Vulcan, is apparently feeling bad for all the people who no longer have homes in the Central District. He is offering to build... well, not build exactly, more like construct... housing for the homeless. He will turn shipping containers (you know, the kind smugglers use to send young men and women around the world into slavery), anyway... he will turn them into houses, with bathrooms, for the homeless. Again our local media give us this wonderful news without background, without historical context. No mention that Vulcan has been party to the displacement of hundreds of low-income families and individuals at Yesler Terrace. The oldest public housing in the country, and the first to be racially integrated, Yesler Terrace has helped thousands of people get their footing during difficult times in their lives. Rather than simply renovating the property to meet modern standards, Seattle Housing Authority partnered with Vulcan to raze the property and build shiny, new, "mixed-use, multi-income" buildings.

Yesler residents were supposedly going to have the opportunity to move back into the community once construction was complete. Have you read all the local articles about where the displaced residents went during construction? How did they hold their sense of community together when they were dispersed? How did the children respond to being moved from their schools temporarily? Are they eager to move again a year or two after being forced to move away? How about the elderly residents... how did this change impact them?

No, you haven't read those articles. They haven't been written. Instead we are handed this narrative about the generosity of our local gazillionaires and their tenderheartedness towards homeless people. We are expected to be grateful that they are acting in a socially responsible way. And some of us will abdicate our own action for theirs: after all, why put out our resources when they are willing to foot the bill.

Our Mayor and City Council are supposed to be representing all of us, paying attention to the long-term vision we hold for ourselves as a community. Homelessness has risen on this mayor's watch. We need to remember that when the next election cycle comes around.

As for the sheer amorality reflected when a group of people can sit in a conference room and decide it's a good idea to put homeless people in rows of storage containers... I can't even begin to address that, it breaks my heart too much. And that they want to put those storage containers in Columbia City, not Phinney Ridge, or Magnolia, or Sandpoint... really?

Former governor Christine Gregoire is spearheading a new project called Challenge Seattle. It is supposed to bring together all of our area's CEOs to solve the major challenges we face. May I suggest a first action for them: a course on the moral implications and responsibilities of power.

As for our local media: a reminder that if it's not investigative it's not journalism, it's just gossip.

Let's Repeal the Second Amendment So We Can Get On With Addressing Gun Violence

by Brian Bergen-Aurand

On March 9, 2018, Florida Governor Rick Scott signed into law a number of restrictions on gun ownership in that state. Earlier in the week, the state legislature had passed the bill to the governor. Within a month of the murder of seventeen students at Marjory Stoneman Douglas High School in Parkland, Florida had enacted some of the measures gun control advocates continue to recommend and demand.

Immediately, the National Rifle Association filed a lawsuit in federal court to overturn the new Florida regulations. NRA lawyers have called for a judge to block Florida's new measures before they take effect.

On March 14, thousands of students, teachers, staff, and allies walked out of classes and off the job for seventeen minutes to remember the murdered Parkland students and continue the protest against gun violence.

The NRA responded to the walk out by tweeting the image of an AR-15 with the caption, "I'll control my own guns, thank you." The act was quickly derided online and off for what many critics saw as its ridiculously callous mocking of the grieving students, mourners, and participants.

On March 24, walks against gun violence took place at different locations around the nation. As the organizers stated, these demonstrations are not just political rallies, but constitute a "march for our lives."

But, even before the walks had begun, the National Rifle Association attacked the proponents of the event. "March For Our Lives is backed by radicals with a history of violent threats, language, and actions," claimed the National Rifle Association in a segment on NRATV on March 21.

The pattern is clear. Repeatedly, we have seen discussion of gun violence and strategies for addressing it hampered and thwarted by gun lobby groups and gun sales associations. Even the limited measures such as those suggested after Parkland (and after the Great Mills High School shooting in Maryland) have been challenged before the conversation begins. Most often, the first and last argument against further movement on gun violence legislation is to cite federal, state, and local guarantees of gun rights.

If we are to move forward on this conversation regarding gun responsibility, then we must remove this hindrance to full, free, and open debate—the second amendment. In no way would repealing the second amendment equal repealing gun ownership across the country. Only three countries in the world have constitutional language favoring the right to bear arms—Mexico, Guatemala, and the United States, according to a November 2017 Business Insider article. Yet, citizens in Canada, South Africa, the United Kingdom, Japan, Pakistan, Jamaica, Panama, and many other countries still own guns. For the most part, their systems are well designed and highly regulated. Yet, private citizens who meet the local criteria may still arm themselves.

Here, I am not calling for the outlawing of guns in the United States; I am calling for rigorous debate and effective action, without the hindrance of the second amendment and the organizations that evoke their interpretations of it to halt the conversation.

I know it is extremely difficult to change the Constitution of the United States of America, and I am glad about that fact. Outside of a few highly regrettable flaws (such as the "punishment" clause of the thirteenth amendment) I think it is an important and valuable document in the history of nation-states.

Amending the Constitution to repeal the second amendment and open a full debate on the best ways to address gun violence across the United States would involve a significant two-step process that could take up to seven years to complete. The procedure is outlined in article five of the Constitution, and the timeframe was established by Congress after the ratification of the eighteenth amendment to the Constitution.

First, either Congress or the States can propose an amendment to the Constitution. Congress can do so with a two-thirds vote in both the House of Representatives and the Senate. The States can do so with a two-thirds vote of their legislatures calling on Congress to hold a constitutional convention.

Second, after the amendment has been proposed, it must be ratified by the States. Either three-fourths of state legislatures or three-fourths of state ratifying conventions must approve the amendment.

Seeing how much this process depends on the States to carry it forward, Washington state, certainly, could take a leadership position in this debate. Our state already has an open conversation about gun rights and gun regulations going as well as a record of balancing those two concerns with regard to our state constitution's own article 1, section 24, which, rather than being absolute in its guarantees, grants and limits gun ownership and use. According to the Giffords Law Center:

> Washington courts have held that the right to bear arms is not absolute and is subject to reasonable regulation by the state under its police power. The Supreme Court of Washington has repeatedly rejected article I, § 24 challenges to state and local firearms regulations. The Courts of Appeals have also followed this approach.

Our state has earned a score of B from the Law Center, which recommends several steps we might take to improve our ranking and further reduce our gun death rate. However, such a model for discussion as we have already developed could add momentum to the larger national movement to reduce gun violence and push us toward a free and unencumbered debate about the path ahead—a path often barred by references to the "protections of the second amendment."

My proposal is not a unique one. In 2013, the editors of *America* magazine proposed repealing the Second Amendment for reasons similar to mine. "The Supreme Court has ruled that whatever the human costs involved, the Second Amendment 'necessarily takes certain policy choices off the table,'" write the authors. In response, they ask if we have not given up too much of our ability to protect ourselves and if it is not time to reclaim our right to act on our own behalf.

Similarly, in 2017 Bret Stephens, writing in the *New York Times*, claimed there is only one way for "Americans who claim to be outraged by gun crimes" to take control of the changes they want to see enacted: "Repeal the Second Amendment."

Last month, Stephens returned to the topic after the Parkland mass shooting. "We need to repeal the Second Amendment because most gun-control legislation is ineffective when most Americans have a guaranteed constitutional right to purchase deadly weaponry in nearly unlimited quantities," he asserted in the *New York Times* again.

Other appeals for repeal have appeared in *Rolling Stone* and *Vanity Fair*.

Thus far, in 2018, the United States has experienced 49 mass shootings, resulting in 3,178 deaths and 5,559 injuries, according to the Gun Violence Archive. That is an average of one mass shooting every 1.6 days. If we continue at this rate, we will have to multiply those numbers by more than four before the year's end.

THE INJUSTICE OF JURY DUTY

by Laura Humpf

In December, the red postcard many dread arrived, summoning me to jury duty. I was intrigued and curious about my first opportunity to serve, and I showed up on a Tuesday morning at 8:00 AM with about 200 other jurors. I walked in and noticed a sea of predominantly white faces like my own. If jury selection is random, I wondered, why isn't 30% of the room people of color, the number of people of color available, according to the King County 2011 census.

The judge came out to give us a "pep talk." He shared how much people learn about the justice system from serving and lamented about never being able to serve himself. He shared a quote from a previous juror who found the experience incredibly rewarding. He then told us the per diem was $10/day, acknowledged that this would not pay for a car to park downtown, and that the per diem had not been raised since the 1950s. He said jury duty was a sacrifice he hoped we would make.

Jury duty did not sound like a sacrifice; it sounded like a luxury. Who can afford this? I soon found out.

100 names were read for a trial that would last over three weeks. My name is called and I pick up my questionnaire. The first question asked if serving would be a substantial hardship, and I shared that as a yoga therapist who is self-employed, I cannot sustain myself on $10/day for three weeks. As I turned in my form, I was behind an older white man. I glanced at his survey and saw, "none" under the hardship question. I, and over half the people called were dismissed due to a substantial hardship. It seemed the few people of color selected were also dismissed.

An older white woman next to me got up and walked out with the other white people to determine the fate of this case. It became clearer to me who has the luxury to serve—white folks with class privilege.

The sixth amendment to the United States Constitution states, "In all criminal prosecutions, the accused shall enjoy the right to a speedy and public trial, by an impartial jury of the State and district wherein the crime shall have been committed, which district shall have been previously ascertained by law, and to be informed of the nature and cause of the accusation; to be confronted with the witnesses against him; to have compulsory process for obtaining witnesses in his favor, and to have the Assistance of Counsel for his defense."

The definition of impartial is "treating all rivals or disputants equally, fair and just."

Yet, how fair is a jury if only those with wealth can serve? How equal is a jury when people of color or young people are not represented in pools, but are disproportionately over-policed and impacted by the criminal justice system? How just is a jury when privilege determines whether you will be able to serve or not?

The pep-talking judge framed jury duty as an opportunity to serve—for the people, by the people. Who is included in "the people" and who is not, though? Jennifer Henderson, who identifies as African-American, middle-class mental health therapist sums up her experience of being summoned with the word "invisible." There were three other visible folks of color in the room and "interestingly enough we were not in either of the groups that were called. We were the ones left behind," she said.

What does a sacrifice mean for a person with wealth and race privilege and for a person without? Does it mean a sacrifice of time with grandkids? Or work piling up? Does sacrifice for someone else mean losing housing? Is it a choice between jury duty or putting food on the table for their children? What does it mean for the person on trial when only people with class and race privilege determine the outcome of the case? What does it mean if the person on trial is a person of color and/or cash poor?

"I wondered about the accused. Who are they? What did they do? How will they be perceived? Did they stand a chance of fairness from this group," Henderson inquired.

The minimum wage in 1961 in Washington State was $1.15 and is now $11.50. In the 60s, a full day of jury duty paid more than a full day's work at minimum wage. Today, it is not equivalent to one hour of minimum wage work in this state.

According to the Washington State Center for Court Research's 2008 Juror Research Project, "jurors who earn more are more likely to be paid by their employer to serve while on jury duty, meaning that those least able to afford jury duty are hit the hardest when they do serve. If juror pay in Washington State today [in 2008] had the same purchasing power as $10 did in 1959, we would pay our jurors $70.14 a day."

According to the Urban Institute, in 2016 white families had seven times more wealth than Black families and five times more than Hispanic families. White people, in general, have more class privilege, which makes serving for $10/day a greater possibility for them.

"In theory it is a great thing to choose an impartial jury. To represent the accused. To give the accused a fair chance so you have multiple opinions and perspectives on the case but it falls far short of what it could be and what it should be in this city," Henderson adds.

The judge explained that we would learn a lot about the justice system if we served. In being a part of the jury selection process, I learned more about the classism and racism embedded in our justice system—and the ways jury duty is yet another example of institutional racism.

What White Marchers Mean for Black Lives Matter

by Marcus Harrison Green

The cries rang out in unison throughout Seattle's Central District.

Black Lives Matter!!!

And as my own voice joined the chorus of hundreds of other marchers, one next to me gave a heavy sigh.

"You can't go anywhere in Seattle without white people," it said. "Seriously, why are all these white folks here?"

Treading through the Central District, we scanned the crowd, taking in the proportion of black to white, feeling every bit the minority in a city two-thirds Caucasian. We were buoys of Hershey afloat in an ivory sea.

Just a year before, it was a different scene. At a march following the death of Eric Garner at the hands of the NYPD, the streets were filled with members of the city's African-American community making a formidable public showing of solidarity against police violence. It was a galvanizing moment early in the Black Lives Matter movement. And, yes, smatterings of white allies were present, but they appeared in a supporting role.

In a very short time, the tide had turned toward crisp irony. Here was a BLM march with a majority of white participants ardently shouting about how much "Black Lives Mattered" in an area that "black life" had been forced to abandon due to high rents and low prospects.

෴

That was almost two years ago, the catalyst for the march the deaths of nine congregants of Emanuel African Methodist Episcopal Church in Charleston, South Carolina. Those innocents had been slaughtered by Dylann Roof, a domestic terrorist who wore his white supremacy on his sleeve.

And while of course these white marchers did not share Roof's politics, and though they meant well, the overwhelming whiteness of the march inspired in me a deep cynicism that poisoned the well of communal warmth. I wondered how many of my white kinfolk were in attendance to simply build their personal brand, this event simply another addition to their "Social Justice CV," along with #BLM Facebook profile pics, effusive Obama sycophancy, and platinum membership to the Ta-Nehisi Coates fan club, all accentuating how "not racist" they were.

Here were hundreds of them flooding past an area once 70 percent black, now less than one-fifth black and "85 percent Black Lives Matter placards" to quote a friend of mine.

That was the last time I deliberately pounded pavement at an organized Black Lives Matter march in Seattle.

I stopped covering BLM marches as a journalist, as well, having grown skeptical of their efficacy.

I do still scroll through the photos, tweet streams, and personal accounts, one blending into the next. What I see are more white faces and fewer black ones. In the past year it has become even more difficult to discern between a march for black lives and one meant to fight climate change, or "Impeach Trump."

At first blush, this development might be cause for jubilation. "Isn't it glorious!" the conventional wisdom declares. "White people are woke and getting it in Seattle."

But are they? And what are the impacts of Black Lives Matter marches where the black lives actually present are outnumbered by white lives?

Could this new dynamic actually be doing more harm than good?

∽

As organizer of the largest Black Lives Matter marches in Seattle since 2014, Mohawk Kuzma has had a front-row seat to the transforming demographics of the BLM movement. He says that my eyes are not deceiving me. There is a noticeable increase of white marchers, one that he says signifies that white Seattleites' long hibernation on Black issues is at its end.

"The reason BLM marches are getting more white is because more white people are waking up and seeing the covert segregation and racial injustice and racism," Kuzma tells me. "We see it on the news every day across the nation."

He draws a connection with the overt displays of racism, from pervasive police killings of blacks to the recent domestic terrorist acts by white supremacists, most recently a school shooting by one in New Mexico.

Kuzma says that when he began organizing he welcomed whatever race, gender, or orientation felt compelled to attend, as long as the marchers understood "that all black lives matter and racial injustice, police brutality, and racism needed to stop."

However, he also recognizes that the increased numbers of white folks is a double-edged sword.

"More white people also brings white ignorance and white fragility," he says. "White people think they have to be respectful during a protest. Sorry, but we as black people don't get respect from anyone, including white people, so why should we be respectful. We are here to get stuff done."

According to artist, educator, and black community organizer Jerrell Davis, the issue of white people showing up to march is subordinate to what's actually facing the black community: black survival. It is a very real concern in a city where more and more black residents are moving to Kent, Des Moines, and other areas of South King County.

"What does it actually mean?" he asks, repeating my question regarding the increasing participation of white Seattleites at BLM marches.

"Does it mean white folks here are more empathetic? Does it mean they're more willing to go to a march they know will be protected by police?"

For Davis, more white marchers equate to an increased police presence at marches. The aura of safety reduces the risk of attending, he says, which leads to nothing more than a march serving as a symbolic act for white people ultimately leaving the racial status quo unchallenged.

"Honestly that shit doesn't shift the culture of this city," he concludes, his black lochs flowing from beneath his green cap.

Davis—who is becoming well known for his socially-conscious, movement-based hip-hop under the name Rell Be Free—has participated in numerous Black Lives Matter marches in Seattle and Philadelphia. And while he sees these marches as a necessity in the broader movement for Black liberation, and an entry point for previously disengaged white people to encounter movement politics, he says more energy needs to shift to the activity between marches.

"[Seattle has] a Race and Social Justice Initiative, but every week there are black people leaving this city because they can't live here. We have a zero detention policy in place, but they're still building a youth detention center. So what good is white people showing up on their own time, when black folks have little time left in this city?"

He views such policies as performative, much like the red, black, and green of the Pan-African flag that is painted on the crosswalks of the Central District. These measures commemorate a once-thriving community, but they do little to empower those who remain. He wonders if the same is happening when white perpetrators of gentrification march in the streets for black lives.

"It's befuddling to me," Davis says. "It's as if some people march as some sort of social justice penance. But do those same people ever ask themselves, 'You know … I'm knowingly moving to this place and it's hurting people, so should I?'"

∽

Concurrent with a rise in white participation is an apparent decrease in the number of black people marching for black lives. It's a shift that doesn't surprise activist Amir Islam. He knows first-hand how exhausting it can be for displaced black folks to travel to Seattle marches.

"Some Black activists are burnt out from marches," he says. "You have to think that a lot of the black community has been pushed out to Auburn, Kent, Des Moines, Puyallup even. … It's hard enough to survive let alone get to your own people for a march."

Islam says he gave up organizing Seattle-area marches about the time I stopped going. He says that marches are simply one thunderbolt in the gathering storm needed to ravage societal racism, and he has chosen to focus his energies on another approach: community development work.

He says he is fine with the increased white presence at Black Lives Matter marches, though he is uncertain of their effectiveness.

"Let white people rally, talk to other white folks, and march for the humanity of black people," he says. "Truthfully, though, it's not like they're doing anything radical like buying up a block of homes to give back to the Duwamish."

Anti-racist whites say they are listening to the concerns of black activists and trying to guard against transgressions while also keeping the door open to more white allies—something that activist Erica Sklar sees as a source of energy for the movement, but one with many potential pitfalls.

"It's two sides to the same coin," says Sklar, an organizer with Anti-racist organization CARW. "The reality of Seattle's population means there's more white folks and could mean more exposure, but white folks need a critical analysis of issues."

That deep analysis includes a raw, unflinching assessment of the role racism has played in shaping our present, and where it has placed white people, relatively to non-whites, in this country.

Sklar, who served as a civilian peacekeeper at Seattle's most recent May Day protest, says she has witnessed white people armed with good intentions but lacking crucial foundational recognition of the social justice movements they aim to serve.

"When you show up the first time [to a march], maybe you don't know who you're accountable to, but you should know by the end," she says. "I think a majority of white folks come to this work with fervor but not a deep analysis. One of the deep tragedies of race in this country is white people are never told that they don't belong somewhere. So they think they belong everywhere."

Such a scenario played out last April when Black Lives Matter Philadelphia decided to host meetings free of white people so that their members could "come together to strategize, organize, heal, and fellowship without the threat of violence and co-optation."

Cue the apoplectic white liberal fury (along with the expected alt-right trolling). Black people, working on black issues, outside of the white gaze for some reason elicited outrage.

It was a situation where black people were actually asking white people for support in the form of trust. Trust to organize and heal, free from prying oversight.

I've heard it myself many times: the white colleague with the gilded heart who just wants to know what they "can do," unsatisfied with my taoist suggestion that "doing nothing" is at times more than enough.

"Sometimes, we as white people have to understand that support means leaving a space," says Sklar.

Fellow white anti-racist organizer Carly Brook says the initial burning desire of many white people to attend a BLM march, particularly after a high-profile killing of a black person by law enforcement, is symptomatic of white folks being "socialized to attend to urgency," without the necessary accountability to the movements they're attempting to assist.

"Seattle has a culture of advocacy, but not organizing for advocates; we try to speak for each other," explains Brook, who organizes with the Seattle chapter of white anti-racist group European Dissent as part of the People's Institute for Survival and Beyond.

She says while she's encouraged about white folks becoming increasingly aware of the acute systems of oppression that black folks face, she echoes Sklar's concern about white people having deeper conversations about what they're truly fighting for.

∽

The stone-cold truth is that in a city where a mayor's race can be won without one single black vote, the social currency possessed by white folks is powerful. Yet, allies must walk a tight-rope between utilizing the privilege society has afforded to them and making sure they're amplifying the work of people of color instead of overshadowing POC efforts. Here too, there is work to be done.

During a coffee meet-up, activist, musician, and organizer Gabriel Teodros told me about the times his anti-racism conversation has been met with curiosity, while that of the attendant white artist was met with moonstruck fascination.

"It's a reality that when you go into a room with a group of white people, they aren't going to pay attention to us in the same way they would another white person, even though we're both saying the exact same thing," says Teodros.

It seems like common sense, but must still be said: Only by listening to those who have a lived experience of oppression that white allies can understand what they are fighting for. But there is an important role for those white voices as well, says Sklar.

"The reality of Seattle's population means that more white folks could mean more exposure for [anti-racist] issues," says Sklar.

The best way to reach white people, after all, is through other white people. Just look at a couple recent surveys: Nationally, 91 percent of white people have social networks exclusively comprising other white people according to a poll by the Public Religion Research Institute, and 57 percent of whites believe "reverse-racism" is widespread. This is why European Dissent and CAR-W encouraged their members to discuss racism with their white family members during the holidays. It might make for awkward dinner conversation, but it is arguably more impactful than marching in the streets.

"It's going to take a lot of holding people we disagree with close. We must keep imagining it's possible. It's going to take lifelong work," Sklar says, adding that people must also engage in these discussions with co-workers, friends, and clergy members.

Those routine interactions are how societal transformations are nourished. For the black activists I spoke with the time to do so is yesterday. If marching in the streets helps get more white people out of their social bubble and engaged with black issues, then, so be it.

"The city is engaged in a conversation of who actually gets to live in the city," says Teodros. "You and I are talking in Seattle today, but it could be Kent tomorrow if we aren't doing the work every day to ensure this community stays here."

In other words: start marching, then take further strides.

White Americans Are Still Confused About Racism—Here's "The Talk" We Need To Have

by Jon Greenberg

Growing up and now living in the predominately white city of Seattle, I've known and worked with countless White Americans. I have yet to meet one White American who has given or received "The Talk."

You know, the one that primarily Black American families have to have with their children to keep them safe from the police—*because of their race*: "Keep your hands open and out in front of you, shut your mouth, be respectful, say 'sir.'"

༄

White Americans have the privilege to grow up without "The Talk," but that doesn't mean they should grow up without a talk.

Perhaps because too many White Americans never get one, they too often get race so wrong.

For one, a recent survey reveals that a startling number of White Americans—55%—believe that they are the targets of discrimination. Other studies have corroborated such high percentages. Important to note about this recent survey is that "a much smaller percentage" of those White Americans say that they actually experienced the discrimination.

Before you start blaming Trump supporters for these results, a pre-election poll of 16,000 Americans revealed that Clinton supporters, too, have some serious work to do. For example, 20% of Clinton supporters described Black Americans as "less intelligent" than White Americans.

Racism is a problem all across the board for White America, even in "progressive" places like Seattle.

Maybe this deep misunderstanding of racism explains why too many White Americans don't lift a finger to stop it. Literally. Most White Americans—67%—refuse to even click to share articles about race on social media.

We White Americans are long past due for a "Talk" of our own. I've even readied some talking points for you.

Before I lay them out, I'd like to note that I'm hardly the first to compile such a list. However, given white peoples' attitudes and inaction on racism, another article certainly can't hurt and could even help.

It's worth adding to this wealth of existing information because many White Americans still hold on to what they think are legitimate reasons to dismiss information about systemic racism against people of Color.

You may think such reasons are valid, too. You might believe that the evidence of systemic racism is "anecdotal," argue that sources are "out of date," or feel skeptical about information from op-eds or radical lefty publications.

So you should know that, for this one article, I'm sticking with numbers, not stories. Also know that, for the most part, I'm citing publications only from the last few years and from mainstream news publications, government or academic studies/data, or coverage of such studies/data from mainstream news publications. As much as possible, I'm staying clear of left-leaning sources like *The Huffington Post*, which initially covered the Trump campaign in its Entertainment section.

While reading, keep two key numbers from the Census in your head:

- 62: the percentage of this country that is White American (not Latinx)
- 13: the percentage of this country that is Black American

If access to institutional power were spread proportionally, 13% of Black Americans and 62% of White Americans would make up any given institution.

Finally, I focus primarily on disparities between Black Americans and White Americans for two reasons. First, the disparities between these demographics are often the most extreme—making them harder to deny. Second, White Americans are most frequently targeting the Black Lives Matter movement in their pushback. Does any data justify this pushback?

Let's examine why it doesn't. Here are the talking points for "The Talk" that White Americans urgently need to have.

1. **PRIMARY AND SECONDARY EDUCATION**

    The U.S. Department of Education recently found that Black preschoolers are 3.6 times more likely to be suspended than White preschoolers. Preschoolers. Representing 19% of preschoolers, Black children make up half of all preschool suspensions.

    And these disparities continue throughout their schooling. Here's data from Seattle Public Schools, even several years after the Department of Education launched an investigation into the district's treatment of Black students.

    Given these disparities, it's no surprise that large gaps in achievement and representation in advanced classes for Black and White students persist.

    And the predominately white teaching force—90% white in Washington state—invariably plays a role. The *Washington Post* reports that "Black students are half as likely as white students to be assigned to gifted programs, even when they have comparably high-test scores." That disparity disappears when the teacher is Black.

2. **HIGHER EDUCATION**

    According to the Pew Research Center, 69% of all bachelor degrees are held by White Americans. While Black enrollment in universities has "skyrocketed" in the past twenty years—despite the bleak disparities of public education—Black Americans make up only 6% of enrollment at "top-tier" universities.

    Census reminder #1: It should be 62% and 13% —not 69% and 6%.

    "The Talk" for White Americans must include an honest discussion about education. The narrative of our educational system as leveler of the playing field doesn't hold up with a racial lens.

3. EMPLOYMENT

Because education level correlates to employment opportunities, educational disparities have narrowed and color-coded the pool of employment applicants. And race continues to matter for those who remain.

The *New York Times* has compiled multiple studies over the past twenty years that *all* confirm that White Americans' race benefits them in the process of gaining employment—like the study from 2009 that found Black applicants without criminal records fared as well in getting hired as White applicants with criminal records.

But I promised more recent research. The *Washington Post* asserts that Black Americans are twice as likely to be unemployed as White Americans—*a statistic that was true back in 1954*. If you include incarcerated Americans, Black Americans are nearly three times as likely to be unemployed.

The disparities extend to household income. According to CNN, the average household income for White Americans is $71,300. For Black Americans? Just $43,300. And they extend to homelessness as well. One study found that, in 2010, Black families were seven times more likely to stay in a homeless shelter than White families.

Not only is the poverty rate of Black Americans (26.2%) more than 2.5 times that of White Americans (10.1%), Black Americans are "much more likely" to live in concentrated poverty, which means they have less access to the coveted schools that drive housing purchases.

"The Talk" for White Americans must include an honest discussion about employment and poverty. The narrative of hard work leading to riches doesn't hold up with a racial lens.

4. CRIMINAL 'JUSTICE' SYSTEM

Since I just mentioned incarceration, let's dig into that pile of data. The Prison Policy Initiative reports that in 2014 Black Americans made up 40% of the incarcerated population in the US; White Americans made up just 39%. (Census reminder #2: 13 and 62, respectively, are the population percentages.)

To frame it another way, Black men are six times more likely to be incarcerated than White men, according to the Pew Research Center. BET confirms that the same is true for Black women when compared to White women. (I could not find data from a mainstream source about incarceration rates of queer women or non-binary people, which is telling.)

But I know those disparities don't convince everyone of institutional racism. After all, Black Americans could commit more crimes, right?

Well, not if you start with drug use. In our federal prisons, 46% are incarcerated because of drug offenses. Yet a 2013 government survey of 67,500 people revealed that White and Black Americans use drugs at similar rates (9.5% and 10.5%, respectively).

Isolate heroin use, and the picture shifts dramatically. The *New York Times* reports that "nearly 90% of those who tried heroin for the first time in the last decade were White."

But the injustice of mass incarceration isn't just about who ultimately gets locked up. Racial disparities pervade every step of the process leading to incarceration (as well as those that follow it).

That includes police stops, police searches, police use of force, arrests, pre-trial incarceration, prosecution charges, conviction rates, prison versus community service sentences, length of sentencing, parole access, hiring rates after incarceration, and voting disenfranchisement. (Okay, that was my one Huffington Post source—but a damn important one.)

Vanity Fair recently compiled eighteen studies on racial bias in law enforcement and concludes, "the research paints a picture of a nation where a citizen's race may well affect their experience with police."

Just as many White people are now arguing that the heroin epidemic is a "disease" and not a crime, we don't have to use the criminal justice system to address "the myriad of social needs" that Black Americans face, as Ta-Nehisi Coates highlights in his short Youtube video for The Atlantic" The Enduring Myth of Black Criminality"

"The Talk" for White Americans must include an honest discussion of a system that, according to Ava DuVernay's documentary "13th," evolved from slavery. The narrative of our system as a "justice" system doesn't hold up with a racial lens.

5. WEALTH

Comparing wealth leads to the most extreme disparities. Here's a new number to remember: sixteen. According to Forbes, a typical White household has sixteen times the wealth of a Black household.

And this is where history matters (and you don't even have to go back very far). *CNNMoney*'s Youtube video, "Wealth: America's other racial divide," is a two minute crash-course on the discriminatory housing practices that played a large role in today's wealth disparities, giving White Americans a head start and only allowing Black Americans into the race when real estate had appreciated beyond an affordable cost for too many.

CNN reports that, based on current trends, "it will take 228 years for black families to accumulate the same amount of wealth" that White Americans have today.

While we like to think of education as the answer to these disparities, new research shows that even the benefits of a college degree come color-coded. According to The New York Times, from 1992-2013, "the median net worth of blacks who finished college dropped nearly 56%." In contrast, the net worth of White Americans who finished college climbed nearly 86%.

"The Talk" for White Americans must include an honest discussion about this country as a meritocracy. That narrative of education as a pathway to social mobility doesn't hold up with a racial lens.

6. HOUSING

The rate of home ownership for White Americans is 73% and for Black Americans is 45%, and is explained in the previously mentioned *CNNMoney* video. Like with the criminal "justice" system, bias is documented in many of the steps in the home-buying process.

Forbes uncovers that Black people tend to receive higher interest rates and that Wells Fargo admitted to pushing Black households into sub-prime mortgages.

The *New York Times* reports that, when applying for conventional mortgages, one in four Black Americans are denied, compared to one in ten for White Americans.

And for those who actually make it to the house hunt, a $9 million study of 28 metropolitan areas found that "[c]ompared with white home-buyers, blacks who inquire about homes listed for sale are made aware of about 17% fewer homes and are shown 18% fewer units."

"The Talk" for White Americans must include an honest discussion about housing discrimination—past and present. The narrative of housing as part of the American dream doesn't hold up with a racial lens.

7. HEALTH

What does systematic racial oppression do to the health of the Black population? A 2012 study—for the most part, before viral videos of police killing Black Americans filled our newsfeeds—found that Black Americans report "experiencing discrimination at significantly higher rates" than other racial or ethnic groups, leading to PTSD-like symptoms—not from war, but from living in the United States.

According to NPR, a social epidemiologist at the University of California, Berkeley, found in studying Black women "that chronic stress from frequent racist encounters is associated with chronic low-grade inflammation—a little like having a low fever all the time."

Unfortunately, if you are Black, your doctor may be ill-equipped to treat you. The Washington Post recently compiled several studies that document racial bias in health care—including one that found "whites are more likely to be prescribed strong pain medications for equivalent ailments." NPR attributes many of these disparities to the "unconscious biases" of the doctors.

"The Talk" for White Americans must include an honest discussion about health care. The narrative of doctors fulfilling their Hippocratic Oath doesn't hold up with a racial lens.

8. Media Representation

Vanity Fair writes that, of the top-grossing films of 2014, 73.1% of the speaking roles went to White Americans, while just 12.5% went to Black Americans. (Reminder #3: 62% and 13%.) This over-representation of White people in Hollywood has led to two straight years of the #OscarsSoWhite hashtag.

Media representation is a category where other groups of Color can fare worse than Black Americans. For example, Latinx Americans—17.6% of the population (some of whom are Black)—make up just 4.9% of speaking roles.

Even though diverse casts translate to box-office success, according to NPR, representation in our media remain stubbornly White—from the cast to the creators.

But numbers are only part of the issue. The types of roles available also matter, and many groups of Color find the menu of opportunities quite limited (with color-coded, lower paychecks to match), which might explain Viola Davis's 2015 Emmy acceptance speech: "The only thing that separates women of color from anyone else is opportunity."

"The Talk" for White Americans must include an honest discussion about the media we consume. With a racial lens, the narratives of some people barely exist.

ᴄᴏ

Given this deluge of data, is it possible that you as a White American are systemically oppressed?

Well, I never want to tell another person what their experience is. After all, that seems to be the primary strategy of All Lives Matter folks and meninists: denying the oppression of others.

Is it possible that a White American remains stuck in concentrated poverty *because of their race*, gets targeted by the police *because of their race*, gets a shitty education *because of their race*, can't get a fair shot at a top university *because of their race*, can't get a fair shake at a good job *because of their race*, can't get access to good housing or health care *because of their race*, and can't find anything to watch aside from *Empire*, *Fresh Off the Boat*, *Master of None*, and *Luke Cage*?

I suppose anything is possible, but it sure as hell doesn't seem likely.

In critiquing the profound anti-blackness throughout this country's history, Robin DiAngelo puts it another way: Black Americans have never had the power to systemically commit the atrocities that White Americans have committed—and continue to commit—against them.

It is not an understanding of reality or history that leads to those high percentages of White Americans who report feeling oppressed.

Far more likely, White Privilege has warped our understanding of our current system—a system that, according to all the data, we desperately and collectively need to break.

"We keep saying the system is broken, and it's not. The system works exactly
the way it's supposed to. So instead of saying 'the system is broken, let's fix
it,' we should be saying 'the system is working, let's break it.'"
~Marc Lamont Hill

We need to break it so that—together—we can rebuild a more just one.

Ultimately, that's "The Talk" that White Americans need to be having.

So, What Do We Do With Youth Who Attempt To Kill?

by Nikkita Oliver and Gyasi Ross

It is true. People harm each other. In our current world this seems an unavoidable inevitability. The certitude of which is frightening for many. This fear often drives the public into the arms of anything that might offer a semblance of protection—like jails or police. Or we just throw money at the problem. This will surely make it go away!

Often the first question asked abolitionists is, "What do we do with people who commit acts of violence such as assault or murder?" The media and politicians sensationalize this question focusing on specific gruesome events to make their point. While this often "wins" out in the court of public opinion, it is really just "fear mongering". This is not to say the fear is unreal. Rather, it is not the whole picture.

If a picture is worth a thousand words, the frame is worth even more. How we choose to "crop" an issue or frame a question impacts the answer.

So, let's assume everything is true. Assume some youth will attempt to kill, but also assume the criminal "justice" system, including jails, courts and probation, increase inequality, do irreparable harm to youth and families, increase the likelihood of recidivism, are not rehabilitative, and do not provide effective prevention. Why do we continue investing in a system that actually increases the likelihood that youth will continue to attempt to kill?

We need to reframe our question. Why not ask, "What do we do with an inequitable and ineffective system that actually perpetuates current negative outcomes and increases the likelihood youth will attempt to kill?"

Politicians love numbers and data, right? A 2013 study of over 35,000 youth in a large urban area found juvenile incarceration decreases the prospect of high school completion and increases the potential of adult incarceration. According to the Justice Policy Initiative crime rates amongst youth are the lowest they have been in 20 years! Yet, the use of juvenile detention is not decreasing at the same rate. Rather, nationally it is increasing with 70 percent of the youth detained being held for nonviolent offenses.

We Seattlites tend to think of Seattle as the great exception. We are not! While there are fewer youth in the King County Youth Jail than ever before, racial disproportionality and the disparate impact on communities of color is skyrocketing. Between 2010 and 2014, King County Juvenile Court filings decreased immensely—felony filings fell 39% and misdemeanors 51%. While felony filings have decreased for all youth the largest beneficiary of this drop remains white youth. Between 2013 and 2014 the felony filings against Black (20%) and Native (17%) youth increased. In their own report KC Youth Justice writes, "… despite an almost 70 percent drop in King County's juvenile detention population since 1999, the racial disproportionality that remains in it has increased to unacceptable levels." Nearly half of the youth subjected to the detention center are Black despite the fact our Black community only makes up a tenth of the County's population.

#NoNewYouthJail (NNYJ) organizers are asking the City of Seattle and Martin Luther King, Jr. County to move towards zero detention of youth. Research shows that jailing youth causes irreparable trauma and increases the likelihood of recidivism. NNYJ organizers believe in justice, accountability, and setting youth up, including youth who commit crimes, to live healthy productive lives in community. Organizers believe in a community where adults take accountability for the inequitable system and institutions we setup and manage. A system which forces certain youth and families into poverty, marginalized and excluded communities, and, ultimately, the school-to-prison pipeline.

Facts. The current in use portion of the King County Youth Detention Center is 25 years old. It is neither "toxic nor cramped" rather it is practically empty. On average in November there were 33 youth jailed in the facility. Yet, the proposed new building is projected to contain 120 beds. The current facility is in need of *some* repairs, but not $210 million worth! King County's own study of the existing facility describes it as "generally in good condition" requiring $795,981 worth of repairs; which is $209,204,019 less than the proposed facility.

People will continue to harm each other; including young folks. It is going to happen and we must have programs, facilities, and communities in place to respond. These programs and facilities should be proportional to the number of young folks who are likely to have contact with these systems, but more importantly must provide a humanizing community-based experience. In reality, we all make mistakes and we all deserve the opportunity to move forward to make different and better choices.

The proposed youth jail is not only wildly disproportionate to the current use of detention in Seattle, but it also increases inequality and the likelihood of harm and trauma. Spending a million to repair the current facility seems an unfortunate inevitability. However, this does not mean we should continue to invest any more than we "have to" in this proven ineffective and unjust system. Honestly, we should be more frightened by a system which keeps us in harm's way, than we are of the *possibility* a youth may attempt to kill.

WHITE SILENCE CAN BE GOLDEN

by Marilee Jolin

On Saturday night, I had the distinct privilege of attending Spectrum Dance Theatre's production of *A Rap on Race*. The script is an adaptation of the 1970 recorded conversation between poet and author James Baldwin and anthropologist Margaret Mead. Baldwin (portrayed by local, Tony-award winning choreographer Donald Byrd) and Mead (played by actress Julie Briskman) sit on a raised platform discussing race in America—their tense and powerful conversation reflected in the evocative movements of the superb dancers below them.

Going in, I had no idea what to expect from this theatre experience. I knew little of the real lives of the two characters, having vaguely heard Mead's name but woefully innocent of Baldwin's literary legacy. Would I be lost without the requisite knowledge of these people? No. In fact, from the moment the two American legends opened their mouths I found myself in the midst of a very familiar and eerily modern-sounding conversation.

This familiarity was both illuminating and disturbing. I can't help but ask with shock and disappointment: are we really at the same place in the discussion of race as in 1970? Have we not progressed in 46 years? Over the course of the 80-minute performance, Baldwin and Mead fall into a well-worn pattern with Baldwin trying to convey the exiling and intolerable experience of being black in the United States while Mead attempts to exonerate herself from blame and, moving quickly past Baldwin's pain, focus the conversation on the future.

After a particularly intense exchange in which Mead dismisses Baldwin's suffering by focusing on her internal beliefs, Byrd finally exclaims, "We've got to make some connection between what you believe and what I've endured!"

In hearing that sentence a light bulb went on for me. The use of those two words *belief* and *experience* illuminated a White person problem that has been plaguing me for months. I realized just how great a distance exists between what White people believe and what People of Color have endured. I realized how much White people sabotage opportunities for true connection by focusing on our beliefs and knowledge at the expense of the lived experience of People of Color.

The reality is this: People of Color have experienced racism and White people have not. Indeed, we cannot. The very nature of racism and power is that those in power cannot experience it. Which leaves us with only knowledge. And when it comes to racism, I am coming to believe more and more strongly, knowledge is not enough. Without personal experience, our knowledge is at best incomplete and at worst quite damaging.

This is a lame illustration, but bear with me. A few hours after the birth of my first daughter, exhausted and upset by her disinterest in breastfeeding, I asked to see a lactation specialist. To my utter shock, the person who showed up to help me learn how to breastfeed was a man! I flat-out refused—told him we were fine and didn't need help. This was a lie. My daughter was not eating and I was scared. But I couldn't stomach the idea of a man trying to help me with this uniquely female, decidedly intimate process. I'm sure he possessed plenty of helpful knowledge. But him *knowing about* breastfeeding was of no interest to me. I needed a connection with someone who had *experienced it.*

I don't mean to imply in any way that breastfeeding and racism are the same or to conflate them. Still, the analogy resonates with me. The amount of distaste and anger I felt toward that male lactation specialist was infinitesimal compared to the fury People of Color must experience when White people show up to conversations about racism with our detached, abstract and rational knowledge.

By focusing on what we believe we are failing to make the connection Baldwin called for. To truly build this necessary connection, we must wrap our heads around the limits of knowledge and stop trying to share our opinions on racism with People of Color. We must recognize that our knowledge is deeply inferior to POC *experience* and our championing of such knowledge harms our relationships and alienates us from the people with whom we most need to connect.

What then can we do? Well, here are a few ideas to get you started:

- Attend an Undoing Racism

  The People's Institute for Survival and Beyond regularly conducts Undoing Racism trainings in Seattle and these trainings should be considered required coursework for all White people. The skilled facilitators at Undoing Racism trainings expertly draw on history, sociology, personal experience and the experiences of the participants to create a safe but challenging environment that enlightens while it humbles, plants seeds with immense potential and builds relationships for further work. If you care at all about issues of race this is an essential step.

- Shut off the Damn Internet and Meet Some Real Life People

  Nothing can compare to personal interaction with other people, particularly when it comes to questions of race. I'm sure there are many different groups having these discussions near you: churches, libraries, schools. European Dissent is a great organization that offers opportunities for White people to meet and discuss race. Take those 15 minutes you might put toward crafting a Facebook comment and use them instead to invite someone to talk in person about such things.

- Don't Offer Your Opinion

  When in conversation about race and something gets your hackles up and you feel like you have to add something, try saying instead: "Tell me more about that." And then really listen. Don't interrupt. In fact, stay silent much longer than is comfortable. When in doubt say, "Tell me more." You might be surprised what you learn—not only about racism but also about yourself.

I also recommend going to see Baldwin and Mead and the incredible Spectrum Dance Company work through these issues with compelling words and provocative movements. *A Rap on Race* plays through May 22nd, 2018 at Seattle Repertory Theatre. You won't regret it.

And, I promise, you won't regret holding your opinions to yourself either. We all have a lot to learn. But when it comes to racism we White people have more to learn than others. And the only way to do it, the only way to build Baldwin's meaningful connection, is to get over our own beliefs and listen, wholeheartedly, to People of Color's experience.

Moving Beyond Juvenile "Super-Predator" Rhetoric

by Dan Ophardt and Marisa Ordonia

Last month, at a private, $500 per-head fundraiser in South Carolina, Black Lives Matter activist Ashley Williams reminded the nation of a 20 year-old statement from then-First Lady Hillary Clinton. Speaking in 1996 in support of the 1994 Violent Crime Control Act and other White House criminal reform, Ms. Clinton said of juvenile crime, "They are not just gangs of kids anymore. They are often the kinds of kids that are called 'super-predators.' No conscience, no empathy. We can talk about why they ended up that way, but first we have to bring them to heel."

This disturbing rhetoric animalizing children was not unique at the time. These words were based on a theory advanced by John Dilulio in a 1995 *Weekly Standard* article, claiming that "On the horizon, therefore, are tens of thousands of severely morally impoverished juvenile super-predators. They are perfectly capable of committing the most heinous acts of physical violence for the most trivial reasons.... So for as long as their youthful energies hold out, they will do what comes 'naturally': murder, rape, rob, assault, burglarize, deal deadly drugs, and get high."

The problem with Mr. Dilulio's super-predator theory and the laws and practices that it fueled is not just that it has had devastating and disproportionate effects on children and communities of color. Its most fundamental problem was that it was not at all correct, as Mr. Dilulio admitted just a few years after publishing it. His predicted cadres of natural-born violent offenders never appeared. Even by the time Mr. Dilulio first stated his theory, the juvenile crime rate had already begun to fall from its peak in 1994, the year before Dilulio's article. In 1996, the overall juvenile arrest rate began to decline and continued to decline every year through 2014, when it was less than half of the rate it was in 1980. This rise and fall mirrored that of the adult arrest rate, and it occurred uniformly across states, whether or not they had tough laws that sent children through the adult criminal justice system. Today, we remain with entire communities devastated by the overcrowding and disproportionate representation in U.S. prisons.

The super-predator theory gained traction at a time when getting tough on crime was already popular. In 1994, the Violent Crime Control and Law Enforcement Act passed with bi-partisan support. It authorized $9.7 billion for federal prisons, created 50 new federal offenses, added a federal three-strikes rule, and effectively eliminated in-prison education funding. It is often credited with being a large part of the cause of today's overly crowded U.S. prisons. Furthermore, the fear instigated by the super-predator theory caused many states to charge more youth as adults instead of handling their offenses in juvenile court. Between 1992 and 1997, 44 states and the District of Columbia passed laws facilitating more transfer of juveniles to adult criminal court.

Much of the justification for sending more youth to the adult criminal justice system relied on the belief that juvenile court was too soft to deter youth from the type of crime predicted by Mr. Dilulio. However, two retrospective studies comparing the increase of prosecuting juveniles in adult criminal courts in Idaho and New York, two states that had passed new "auto-decline" laws to transfer jurisdiction of more juvenile charges to adult criminal court, showed no evidence of general deterrence of juvenile crime in comparison to similar states around them that had not passed similar auto-decline laws. Furthermore, a study in Florida in the mid-1990s, showed evidence that increased transfer of juveniles to adult court actually promoted recidivism, rather than deterring it.

A more recent study in Washington by the Washington State Institute for Public Policy, completed in 2014 and using data going back to 1994, compared the recidivism of youth charged in juvenile court to youth who were sent to adult criminal court. The study found a statistically significant correlation between charging youth as adults and future crime. For those 20 years studied, prosecuting youth in adult criminal court did not have a deterrent effect, but rather increased recidivism, costing taxpayers approximately $82,824 extra per youth charged in criminal court.

Youth and communities of color have borne a greater share of the harsher treatment and increased criminalization of youth. In 2013, almost 75% of youth automatically transferred to adult criminal court in Washington were Black or Latino. For comparison, youth of color made up only 34% of Washington's general age 10-17 population. In King County, Black youth make up about 10% of the age 10-17 population, but accounted for over 58% of admissions to secure detention in 2015. These stark numbers have led many community members to the conclusion that ending youth incarceration is the only way to end racial disproportionality in the juvenile justice system.

Yet in response to this call for a different approach, we have heard all-to-familiar rhetoric from our elected officials. Statements like an end to youth incarceration "can only happen when there is no one under the age of 18 committing rape, robbery and murder," and highlighting youth charged with "shooting someone multiple times, robbery at gunpoint or rape," invoke the imagery of the juvenile super-predator and a fear-based reaction. While it remains a fact that a small number of youth do commit very serious crimes, it is also a fact that, last year, less than 17% of the youth admitted to King County juvenile detention were charged with violent offenses.

Right now, King County has a chance to use data, research, and the input of those most affected by the juvenile justice system to adopt policies and practices that can work to rebuild from the devastation caused by the over-criminalization of youth and people of color during the super-predator and tough on crime era. Using the money from the Best Starts for Kids Levy, and the Mental Illness and Drug Dependency (MIDD) sales tax, King County should follow the City of Seattle's lead and invest in identifying, implementing, and sustaining community-based supports and alternatives to detention.

Successful alternative programs exist across the country, as documented in the Safely Home report, and, recently, in a *Seattle Times* article that compares Connecticut's approach to juvenile justice to Washington's approach. We know that the use of juvenile detention leads to negative outcomes for youth and communities, and we must move away from a system that was built on unsubstantiated fear and designed to bring youth of color to heel.

While it appears that Ms. Clinton's 20-year old statement was only a short moment of political liability in a long marathon of an election season, it should stand as a bigger reminder to us. If Ashley Williams' quiet protest at that swanky fundraiser last month does nothing else, let it remind us of the dangerous power of rhetoric to often cloud good judgment and science.

Ending Systemic Racism Can Begin With Seattle

by Marcus Harrison Green

Editor's Note: The following is the transcript of a speech given to City of Seattle employees at the Office of Civil Right's Race and Social Justice Initiative Summit on Thursday March 24th, 2017.

Good morning,

In preparation for this speech today, as any good journalist would do, I thought I'd solicit a wide array of opinions on our city's Race and Social Justice Initiative (RSJI). I couldn't think of any place better to pull them from than the people who live in my community of South Seattle. For those who have never, or rarely ever, ventured south of the I-90 corridor, that's the place that actually harbors all that mythical diversity we trumpet in this city.

My interactions there, which the individuals I spoke with allowed me to share, told me everything I needed to know about our city's commitment to racial and social justice.

The first person I spoke with was a white male who had recently moved to the area from Green Lake. As a former city worker, he could recite the credo of the Race and Social Justice Initiative ad nauseum. He bragged about it how much it advertised Seattle as indeed being America's most progressive city; one shining brightly in an otherwise dimly lit country.

He was proud that the RSJI endured attacks from Fox News, and welcomed the onslaught of venom poured on the city including it being called a bulwark of left lunacy and white guilt run amok. (He literally seemed on the verge of fervently chanting our city's name, like Trump supporters chant USA at the sniff of oxygen).

But then I spoke to others…

I talked to young Black man, confined to a wheelchair, paralyzed from the waist down. When I asked him about RSJI, his reply was a lot less glowing.

It was hard for him to fathom the city's oath that every decision it makes has a community's best interest at heart, because he was in the process of being evicted from the apartment he'd lived in for the past 7 years. His disability check could no longer cover his rent, which had nearly doubled in the past year. He asked why, if his community's best interest was really taken into account by our city's policies, why then was the basis for our affordable housing dictated by the city's overall median income of a little over $71,000? Why was it not instead determined at a more micro-level for neighborhoods, such as the one he lived in near Rainier Beach, where many residents made less than 30,000 a year?

The next person I spoke with was a young transgender woman of color who had difficulty buying into the fact that Seattle Public Schools, just like our city, had declared a commitment to racial equity. She had just been suspended from her school for the second time in as many months, left to fall further and further behind in her academic work, because her teacher found fault with her "tone of voice." Not that she was in any hurry to return to a place where she felt unwelcomed and persecuted because of who she was.

And it was tough for a Latino grandmother I sat down with, who is raising her five grand children on nothing but a social security check and food stamps in the fourth richest city in the nation, to fully embrace Seattle's message of racial and social equity, as her economic plight was so dire that she made the choice to defy her Catholic faith in taking one of her grandchildren for an abortion because there was no way to afford to feed one more mouth.

What they saw on the ground was hard to square with our city's towering claims that it strives to create racial and social equity.

And when I brought it to their attention, that RSJI gives the City a way to suggest, stress, and emphasize what actions City departments and lawmakers can take, and that the City could and should influence the school district, I was met with the same answer.

Then, why doesn't it?

If our city affirmed, and shouted, and proclaimed that it was working to end racial and social inequity, why would it not submit on every level to an initiative that can assist with that objective?

Because the words touted so often by our city leaders that speak to Seattle's commitment to justice for all of its residents, as beautiful as they may be, act to many as mascara to cover up our blemishes, and when it wears off, what remains is a reality that is unbearable without a concealer.

Because what we see when we look into the mirror is a reflection of the reality that in a society where racism has been baked so solidly into its core, there is no portion of that society that can be naive enough to believe it can escape bigotry's clutches if the weapons used to combat structural racism are wielded only selectively, and without force.

The racial and social disparities that continue to exist in education, in employment, and police interactions in this most liberal of cities is testament to that.

I know that many of you sit here, people who are change agents, people who have and continue to exhaust your voice, and your energy, and your emotion behind this initiative.

I know that you keep banging your head against the juggernaut that is city bureaucracy, only to be left bleeding, as you run the very real risk of losing your job should you bang too hard.

I know that this happens even with the civic innovations and victories our Race and Social Justice Initiative has produced—such as requiring that departments use the Racial Equity Toolkit at least 4 times each year, if not more, and rallying departments to take concrete steps, now, so we can actually have Zero Detention for the youth of this city.

Because in a city where officials were unable to foresee the uproar from communities of color at the construction of detention center that disproportionality imprisons their youth, were unable to discern the impact of roadwork on businesses on the 23rd Avenue corridor, and were unable to anticipate the fury from proposing a blanket closure of East African businesses, it doesn't appear that every branch or our City government is beholden to its declared intentions.

I know you, as city employees, don't have it easy. You must serve as the unwilling recipients of rage spirals. You encounter colleagues daily who have limited patience in engaging around racial justice because it adds one more thing on a workload that already runneth over. You often commit no errors and still fail. There are times you must feel like Sisyphus in his futile attempt to push his bolder up the hill, only to have it roll back down.

And what else can I give, you ask?

More.

More is what the young man, the student, and the grandmother I mentioned earlier are asking for, more from you seated here, and especially from the ones who are unfortunately not here.

Because you are the first point of contact for the marginalized and discriminated against in this city, you provide a safety net for those who have nothing else to fall back on. They depend on our City's services and governance more than anyone else. And the people in those communities are increasingly the exact demographic of those cast aside in the rest of this country.

And you have the opportunity to grant those demands.

They demand that you contemplate yourself and your actions while working at the City. No matter how fervently you say you adhere to the principles of equity and justice, they demand that you search inside yourself to ask, "how am I culpable in a system that continues to produce racial inequities in our city no better than anywhere else?"

They demand that this pursuit of race and justice and equity not be left at a 9 to 5 job, but be an ever present companion in your life.

They demand that you not see yourself simply an ally in racial justice organizing, but as an accomplice, who has just as much investment in dismantling a racist structure as anyone else.

They demand that even when you look at our policies and practices through a supposedly racial justice lens you are sensitive to the fact that the image you see can still remain murky because of ignorance.

They demand that while you at the City may set the table, what is selected on the menu for dinner should be prepared by those communities you say you serve.

They demand that the best assessment delivered by a racial equity analysis comes not from a calculated evaluation, but from the judgment of our City's behavior toward communities of color as experienced by those very communities.

They demand that you value your ability to listen more than you do speaking.

As a friend recently told me, it means nothing to be the first City to implement a RSJI. But it means a lot to be the City that uses it as an effective tool to help our communities craft their own destinies.

They demand a lot. I know. But they do so because a lot is still needed.

And yes, I know it can be overwhelming.

And yes, I know that it will require creativity, an ability to push the envelope even harder than some of you do now.

But I also know that is the only way RSJI will truly ever make a difference in this city. That is the only way it will be more than just another noble cause that marches slowly towards a death caused by ineffectiveness.

You have even reason to throw up your hands, and say, "I can't." And to go on with the status quo, and do the bare minimum required of you in your position, to never seek to expand your empathy or knowledge base farther than your own understanding of issues, because to do the opposite, especially as a City employee at times, takes herculean heaps of courage and tenacity.

But, as my mother tells me: In this world that is not fair, and not perfect, and will never be Utopian... in this world where people receive privileges due to a stroke of luck at birth because of their gender, race, and class, it is not your fault that you are born into it as it is... but it is absolutely your fault if you leave it that way when you depart from it.

This applies to all of us. For those in positions of public service, as you are, it should spark the questions most important to your position: Why am I here? and Who do I serve?

Now, I don't want to give off the impression that I come from a place of high authority. I come from a place of experience.

I failed to answer those questions the way I should have, by not doing my job as a journalist serving the under-served in this city, including the Black community.

You see, someone in my life, who I love a great deal, was the victim of rape when she was eight years old. And as we grew up together, I witnessed firsthand the effects of that incident that still plague her life. There's not a month she doesn't contemplate ending it.

So even though I'm an atheist, the theology of hell has always been an appealing one, for the sole reason that I believe rapists should have a permanent residence there.

But when my community asked me to cover and aggressively investigate, the killing of Che Taylor, the African American man killed by SPD officers in North Seattle who was convicted of sexual assault more than two decades ago, I ignored them. I chose not to even send a reporter to cover it.

I ignored them when they asked, why aren't you doing more? I ignored them when they asked me to overcome my own prejudices so that I could focus not on an injustice done once by a man, but the justice that needed to be afforded him in this present day. I ignored them when they said we need you to serve us, and not yourself, for the sole reason that that is what you claim to do.

I chose. And I failed them, by not listening to them. I chose to fail them because in my shortsightedness I believed that all the sleep-deprived nights writing articles, all the creditability I had amassed with my community, all the work I had done pushing myself to the point of exhaustion with being a non-profit new source, I thought gave me cart blanche to not be vigilant, to not be accountable.

I've learned from that experience. It is vigilance to the values you claim to embody that keeps you moving in this work. It is accountability to those you fight for that fuels you despite mental and physical fatigue, and frustration. It affords you an answer to the questions: Why am I here? and Who do I serve?

Today, you are here, some of you by choice, some of you by requirement, but regardless, those questions are before you. They will be before you long after you leave this building today and the emotion spurred from your speakers and the workshops you attend has long been extinguished. Those questions will be with you tomorrow at your Department meetings, and the day after when you receive a phone call from an impassioned city resident at their wit's end. They'll be with you when you're seated at the table with power, and it comes your turn to speak.

They will be with you the next time you sit down with another City agency or department and you're tempted to see a bona fide collaboration with them around matters of race and social justice as optional, as opposed to necessary, to achieve Seattle's stated goal.

And your answer to those questions as an individual, as a City, as a department, as a mayor, as a superintendent, as an aide, as a policy-maker, as a program manager, as a <u>councilmember</u> will speak with a magnitude that reverberates through this city's halls, and its streets and its classrooms, and the lives of its residents.

It is that answer that allows us to truly do what has never been done before in this country: To build a city that has destroyed and dismantled the mechanisms of racism, a city that behaves as a new Athens, a metropolis that awakens our world to a new society and advanced democracy.

I hope you locate that answer, and I hope it's the right one, because there is a city full of people eagerly awaiting your response.

A BILLIONAIRE'S BURDEN: ANGRY VOTERS AND THE MAKING OF A PERFECT WORLD

by Fathi Karshie

'Go send your sons to exile
To serve your captives' need
To wait in heavy harness
On fluttered folk and wild—
Your new-caught, sullen peoples,
Half devil and half child
Take up the White Man's burden'
~Rudyard Kipling

Anger has been touted for Trump's logic-defying political success, underscored by his victories in both the Super Tuesday and Saturday contests. Indications are that, even former Obama voters are now turning to Trump because he, apparently, speaks to their anger.

'Foreign born' America's first Black president, Rapist Mexicans, pariah Muslims and exuberant arrogance sum up the supposed anger now marking the road leading to the White House. Anger! Is it?

To the contrary, because this so-called anger can be traced to the election of President Barack Hussein Obama, it may in fact be Fear. Fear of success of American Civil Rights: by those who see, in these successes, diminished expectations of their own privileges. Thus, guised as defenders of everything native, these fear-mongers are 'angrily' planning to take 'America back.' From whom, to who, or where to, seems to be a tumult strategically avoided by tube and main-stream media.

Yet, considering the various political gaffs that have elevated Mr. Trump's political life, one wonders. Not only at why someone, who for example voted for Obama—would flip backwards and embrace Trump as the man who speaks to this anger but also at how the racism present in the political lingua passes for political bravado.

BIRTHERS: PRESIDENT OBAMA AND THE ANGRY VOTERS.

Though arguments presented to pry into Obama's citizenship were guised as legitimate constitutional queries, the flippancy involved is nonetheless conspicuous. At its core lies the question: how a black 'foreign born native,' a 'Jump Jim Crow' prospector—cowardly and minstrelsy—infiltrated and dethroned the de-facto gene-rulers?

Obama's ascendency symbolizes the culmination of America's Constitutional genius—the principle, 'We hold these truths to be self-evident, that all men are created equal...,' as it gives context to the politics of Anger/Fear. Obama, this climatic symbol of U.S. constitutional historicity—the story of America's civil and rights struggles—may in fact be its cursed child. Obama's paradoxical blessing may as well be Trump's. He came into office by galvanizing, as it were, angry voters; Trump may as well overrun Obama's making, as it seems, by use of the same—angry voters.

Yet, unlike Mr. Trump President Obama is confronted with his own ontology—his half-ness and otherness. Born to a black Kenyan 'foreign Muslim' father and a 'native' Caucasian American atheist mother, his identity obstructs his claims: to religion and region—or rather to Christianity and America.

Presenting us with the dilemma of meshing the foreign with the native— the black with the white, the Islamic with the atheist. All made possible, according President Obama, only in the American context. The American context being the constitutional narrative context: the medium upon which American political battles of slavery, anti-slavery, citizenship and rights are staged. Meanwhile, making his persona easy a target by those positioned as the 'true natives' and street sentinels of the American constitutional narrative.

At the center of this: foreign is bad, and native is patriotic simplistic political opportunism lies, a ruffianism that must be resisted. For according to Micheal Neocosmos, this is the very reason why post-apartheid South Africa is a basket of racial unrest. The absurdity of the 'foreigner native and native foreigner,' he observes, lies in 'state politics': which defines labor strategically by use of politics of exclusion. The foreign native—is that similar/familiar 'other' who is viewed by the 'native' as the unjustified claimant to national resources. The native on the other hand is not only a legally defined political entity but also self-identifies, according to Mamdani, as the 'expropriated'.

It is at this cusp, of law and desire, that the so called anger/fear of the 'native' is materialized and Trump, as the defender of the patria, made possible. Not necessarily because he is any more American than president Obama but because of his privileged position; not as billionaire but rather as the obscure 'native'. Whose identity hails from and is thus traceable through obscurity, but certainly through faith and skin color to its 'founders'. This has made politics a desire's play. A means to purge the presidency of its impurities: of halfness and otherness. Thus positioned as America's sentinels, these so called natives' envision a 'perfect world'—without the 'other'. The implications for this are however, extreme and deleterious.

Trump, his excluding casino world view:

"And he had his men load his rifles, and he lined up the 50 people, and they shot 49 of those people, and the 50th person, he said; 'you go back to your people and you tell them what happened.'" ~Trump: cites a fabricated bloody ethnic cleansing story, to a cheering SC audience.

Trump, besides his gory wishes, is an entertainer, a real estate investor, a casino builder, a republican-party presidential candidate who believes America should be run like—not just as any, but *his* company. The republican party is 89% self-identified as non-Hispanic white, with 61% of its affiliates saying they are angry and irked by current events. At 60% gun ownership, 73% of Republicans also say their party is doing them no good. And if 2014 elections are indications the party's movers are 65 or older. One desperately hopes nostalgia to be at play. But, 53% of republicans believe that, as of November 2015, President Obama to have precipitated unemployment. And contrary to stats, that republican counties consume more food stamps, republican leaders tout America's first black president as a socialist dictator, and a food stamp president.

A HISTORY

Bauman Zygmunt, someone I had the pleasure meeting a few years ago, in his seminal work on the holocaust—'Modernity and the Holocaust' helps us contemplate and visualize what this new political swagger may hold. To begin with, for him the West is engaged in intellectual self-delusion, by assuming the Holocaust un-imaginable in today's world.

To the contrary, he argues that the social features that made the Holocaust possible have not disappeared to the extent that one can't be certain of the 'ripeness' of conditions of such an event. When it happened, no one expected it. And since Hitler's ideological vision—his genocide project was built on desire to control and manipulate, the potential is as real.

At its core, genocide is a product of modern ideology combined with absolute power with access to exacting bureaucracy—and resource. Grounded in a bureaucratic hierarchy, 'akin to that of a subordinate group within a normal power structure' the genocide project touts a 'perfect world' before it consumes its foot soldiers. For him [Zygmunt?] neither Stalin nor Hitler killed to capture territory but on the contrary they killed to manufacture a 'perfect world'.

'I could stand in the middle of 5th Ave and shoot somebody' and not lose a voter; ~Trump says to his exuberant followers.

CONTEXTUALIZING BAUMAN

At a time when scholars are decrying a New Jim Crow—the reversal of civil right gains as demonstrated in the arrests of millions of blacks for minor crimes: acts geared toward denying basic human rights and marginalization. And at a time when, globally, one in every 122 humans is either a refugee, internally displaced, or seeking asylum, one is compelled to ask:

Where is America heading, subsumed by an exuberant crowd led by an arrogantly exuberant rich man, who boasts of having circumvented U.S. laws to catapult himself to richness? While openly insulting a sitting president and talking of deporting Mexicans and banning Muslims all without due process of law?

America is not a real estate. Not a casino. Not a business enterprise. Not a parlor. It is the land of laws and the many; the refugee, the immigrant, the wretched and the brightest.

Read!

> *Give me your tired, your poor,*
> *Your huddled masses yearning to breathe free,*
> *The wretched refuse of your teeming shore.*
> *Send these, the homeless, tempest-tost to me,*
> *I lift my lamp beside the golden door!*
>
> ~ 'The New Colossus' by Emma Lazarus
> On Pedestal of the Statue of Liberty

VIOLENCE IN A NON-VIOLENT WORLD

by Ijeoma Oluo

Like many black children, I was raised with tales of the great Rev. Dr. Martin Luther King Jr. Much of that narrative—at home, in school, in television and in film—centered around Dr. King's commitment to nonviolence in his fight for racial equality.

He was a *peaceful man*, people said, *no matter what, he never struck back.* As I became older, my image of the great Dr. King became more nuanced. I started to see him as more than a man with a dream, as more than a man who didn't strike back. But for many, and for much of the broader narrative of our culture, Dr. King has remained little more than a gentle man with a dream.

Dr. King wouldn't have been that demanding, people say. MLK wouldn't have been so angry. He was a nonviolent man, remember?

And as this past year has had us debating whether or not, in 2017 and 2018, it is OK to punch Nazis, and whether or not Black Lives Matter marches are terrorist acts, the idea of Martin Luther King as the paragon of peaceful protest is invoked more than ever.

But what was nonviolence, really, to Dr. King? Was that all he was? Was peace his only goal?

At a time when those marching to protest the extrajudicial killings of black men, women and children are called thugs; at a time when swastikas are being spray-painted on local synagogues and schools; at a time when families are being torn apart to satisfy the desires of a xenophobic voting base; at a time when armies of anonymous strangers can find you online and tell you that they hope you die without any recourse, while discussing the issue of white privilege will have you banned from social media, can we can look at the work of Dr. King and look at the world we live in today, and ask:

What is violence in 2018? And in this new world, what does nonviolence actually look like?

MLK would be ashamed of you. When I hear these words from someone trying to silence my fight for racial justice and equality, it feels like a body blow. This is not the pain of shame or regret. This is the pain of something that I deeply love—and I deeply love the life and legacy of Dr. King—being abused.

Dr. King was a brilliant leader, a loving husband and father, a man of great faith. But he was, first and foremost, a human being, a man with very human thoughts and feelings, successes and failures. I also heard he was *really* funny.

In his autobiography, he wrote of his early experiences with the violence of racism—both emotional and physical violence. He described many times the anger he felt at experiencing such inhumane treatment. That anger that motivated him to act, just as his father's anger at watching his father before him suffer the injustices of racism, motivated him to leave sharecropping, finish his education and become a minister.

It was after the success of the Montgomery bus boycott that Dr. King came to the teachings of Mahatma Gandhi and the deliberate practice of nonviolence. It was the success of Gandhi's tactics that first drew him in, and he quickly found that the principles of nonviolent resistance also suited his morals and commitment to loving his neighbor. He became convinced that nonviolence was not only the most effective way to combat oppression, it was the only way to do so without becoming an oppressor in your own right in victory.

As Dr. King said, "Nonviolence is the answer to the crucial political and moral question of our time: the need for man to overcome oppression and violence without resorting to oppression and violence. Man must evolve for all human conflict a method which rejects revenge, aggression and retaliation."

But Dr. King's commitment to nonviolence was not a commitment to passivity. It was a commitment to direct confrontation with the violence of oppression. And Dr. King recognized that violence beyond the physical.

In responding to the outcry over rioting of angry and frustrated black youth, Dr. King pushed back against the idea that riots were the violence that society needed to be outraged over. He said:

"Day-in and day-out he violates welfare laws to deprive the poor of their meager allotments; he flagrantly violates building codes and regulations; his police make a mockery of law; and he violates laws on equal employment and education and the provisions for civic services. The slums are the handiwork of a vicious system of the white society; Negroes live in them but do not make them any more than a prisoner makes a prison."

While Dr. King was committed to a life and mission of nonviolence, this does not mean that everyone saw his actions as peaceful. And I think it is important to remember that while King and millions of other black people endured physical, financial and emotional abuse at the hands of white supremacy, it was *his* direct action to confront that oppression that was labeled too destructive, aggressive and even violent. So much so that he was labeled an "enemy of the state" by the FBI.

Sitting in a Birmingham jail, being kept in solitary confinement for leading peaceful resistance to racial segregation, Dr. King decided to respond to white preachers who had chastised him for such "untimely" and "extreme" actions. He said:

"You deplore the demonstrations that are presently taking place in Birmingham. But I am sorry that your statement did not express a similar concern for the conditions that brought the demonstrations into being. I am sure that each of you would want to go beyond the superficial social analyst who looks merely at effects, and does not grapple with underlying causes. I would not hesitate to say that it is unfortunate that so-called demonstrations are taking place in Birmingham at this time, but I would say in more emphatic terms that it is even more unfortunate that the white power structure of this city left the Negro community with no other alternative."

Throughout his work, Dr. King was blamed for "inciting" the violence that met him and fellow protesters in the streets. And as black people throughout the country joined his fight, it was the dissatisfaction of black Americans with the abuses against them that became the main problem for many white Americans.

It is said that even Robert Kennedy, in a moment of frustration over the rising protests of black Americans, exclaimed to his brother, then-President John F. Kennedy: "Negroes are now just antagonistic and mad and they're going to be mad at everything. You can't talk to them. My friends all say [even] the Negro maids and servants are getting antagonistic."

And even now, in 2018, the complaint of Robert Kennedy sounds familiar, doesn't it? Are not those of us marching for black lives also labeled as irrationally angry? Is not our anger over systemic poverty, job discrimination and lack of representation also viewed by many as the bigger threat to society than the abuse and oppression that we face?

What do we face?

Recently there has been rising concern in the medical and scientific community over an issue that has been of extreme concern to the black community for many years: the alarmingly high maternal death rate of black women. As doctors and scientists have looked at why black mothers are dying at three times the rate of white mothers, many have come to see that evidence points to one possible major contributor: racism.

Not just the racism of doctors who do not listen to black patients, who do not believe their pain. Not just the racism behind lower levels of access to preventative care, balanced nutrition and safe and stable housing. Doctors and researchers are pointing to the long-term cumulative emotional effects of living with systemic racism — effects that poison both the body and mind.

This is the fear at every traffic stop. This is the struggle to find out why your child has been sent to juvenile detention by the educators that are supposed to nurture and protect them. This is the pain of smiling through countless office jokes that serve up your humanity for laughs. This is the struggle to pay rising rents while working a job that doesn't think you are management material, and knowing that a bank will never give you a mortgage.

And as we march in the streets to save our kin from state violence, we are called thugs. When we fight for better representation, we are called greedy. When we demand clean drinking water, we are called impatient.

And yet we still fight. And as was done throughout our entire history of struggle, many try to dismiss us. Many say that the real problem is that we are so angry.

Why are you so angry? Dr. King wasn't angry. Be more like him.

Dr. King was a man of love. His love was oceans deep and wide. This was love not only rooted in his faith, but in his community, his family and his people. And all of Dr. King's life he saw those that he loved so much abused, degraded and killed by their own nation. And when he saw that, he was angry.

When he was 14 and forced to give up his seat on a bus and stand for a 90-mile bus ride because a white man had entered the bus and decided that seat was going to be his, Dr. King was angry. When he saw peaceful protesters brutalized by fire hoses and police dogs, he was angry. And when he saw the light go out of the eyes of his brothers and sisters when they gave up hope of ever achieving any measure of success, security or safety in this society, he was very angry.

When Dr. King led his peaceful demonstrations in Birmingham and was jailed, and witnessed his friends and fellow activists who were also arrested for their peaceful protest abused by cops, and then he received word that he had been condemned by white church leaders for supposedly inciting this mistreatment—when he heard of these church leaders praising the police who had abused him and his brothers and sisters for maintaining "order," he was angry.

He wrote to them, "I wish you had commended the Negro sit-inners and demonstrators of Birmingham for their sublime courage, their willingness to suffer and their amazing discipline in the midst of the most inhuman provocation. One day the South will recognize its real heroes."

Now I don't know if you all caught that, but that's "black preacher sending a long letter that names names and will tell you who you are but in a way that will still get published"—angry.

This is not anger over an insult or snub, this is not anger over a dispute or spurned pride. This was an anger born from love. Righteous, pure love. This is an anger that fights to keep love, and those that you love, alive.

Dr. King wrote about his relationship with anger as he reached out to those church leaders who refused to see exactly what he and so many others were fighting for:

"I have not said to my people, 'get rid of your discontent.' But I have tried to say that this normal and healthy discontent can be channelized through the creative outlet of nonviolent direct action. Now, this approach is being dismissed as extremist.

I must admit that I was initially disappointed in being so categorized. But as I continue to think about the matter I gradually gained a bit of satisfaction from being considered an extremist. Was not Jesus an extremist in love?"

Dr. King was angry, but he worked hard to never forget why. He was angry because he loved. And because he loved, he moved mountains.

When you see students protesting when their local school hosts peddlers of hate, bigotry and violence with open arms, and you wonder why they are so angry, I can tell you. They are angry because the racism, anti-semitism, Islamophobia and transmisogyny being hosted by the institutions charged with nourishing and educating them is doing them real harm.

And they love themselves, and they love each other.

When you see people of color demanding better representation in films, movies, novels, history books, and you wonder why they are so angry, I can tell you. Because when I take my young son to see a movie and nobody looks like him, he is told that he doesn't exist. He is not a hero and he is not worth saving. He is not slated for adventure or greatness. His story isn't worth being told. His dreams aren't worth having.

And when he asks me why there are no brown people in this movie, just like in the last movie and the one before that, when I see him limiting his dreams to what society has told him is the best he, as a boy who does not exist in our tales of greatness, can hope for, I am angry. Because I love him.

I am angry. My brothers are angry. My sister is angry. Many of you are also angry. There is a lot to be angry about.

We are angry at the countless ways that those that we love are being harmed every day.

When people are trying to dismiss your anger, when they try to fault your anger. When they try to treat your anger over violence being done against you and those you love as violence itself, and they invoke the name of Dr. King and his commitment to nonviolence in an attempt to shame you, ask them this: *How do you define violence?*

What I am fighting for, what we are all fighting for, is for a life of non-violence. Not only freedom from physical violence. A life free from the all-encompassing violence of systemic oppression. We are fighting for freedom from the violence of the school-to-prison pipeline, from the violence of food deserts, from the violence of undrinkable water, from the violence of teacher bias.

And those who would envision themselves as allied with black Americans, Asian Americans, Latinx Americans, Indigenous Americans, Pacific Islanders and more at the crosshairs of white supremacy. Those who would envision themselves as allied with Dr. King's commitment to nonviolence must join us in our commitment to fight the violence of a discriminatory justice system, to fight the violence of the racial bias of our medical system, to fight the violence of systemic poverty, to fight the violence of erasure.

And to fight the violence of taking our beloved heroes and community leaders and reducing them to little more than a speech about a dream in order to further diminish us all.

We fight this harm—you fight this harm—because you love. You love your kin, your community, your people, and you love your humanity. You love so much that even when all seems against you, even when hate and bigotry has been voted into our highest offices of government—you are still here. You are angry and tired and hurting—and you are still here.

Because you love.

And when it seems to be too much. When the harm and the anger over that harm threaten to overwhelm you, threaten to turn you into someone you do not want to be, reach in deep and find the love at the heart of it all. Or better yet, don't reach in, reach out.

The love is right in front of you, it's right next to you, in this room. This community is why. This is what you are fighting for.

Continue to fight. Continue to work to deconstruct the everyday violences that threaten those you love. And while we fight, let's remember the love that guides us. Let's fight together, but let's also take time to care for each other and heal each other. To nourish the love that will nourish us.

And know that our fight is as righteous and as true as Dr. King's was. Because it is the same fight. And it is the same fight because it is the same love. It is the same love he had for us and still has for us. A love that cannot be extinguished. And as long as it exists, so does the fuel to the fire that we need to one day reach the future that was beyond even the dreams of our most iconic dreamer.

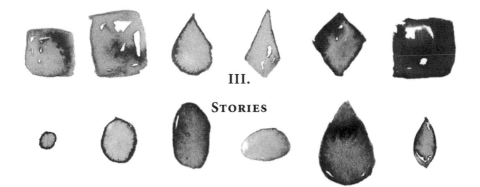

III.

STORIES

One Man's Fight to Free His Son from America's Incarceration Addiction

by Marcus Harrison Green

Like almost every night, Bill Austin awakens to screams.

Nathan is trapped in another nightmare.

Bill leaps from his bed and rushes down the hallway. He nearly rips the handle off the door of his son's room to find the 38-year-old in a familiar state: fighting demons born during a decade in prison.

The images that flood his son's mind are recurring, says the 64-year-old. Gray cell walls collapse in, death drips from the mouths of sadistic cellmates, and images appear of his body pummeled and bathed in blood.

Bill dashes to Nathan's bedside, and shakes him from the grip of a chaotic slumber. "Nathan, wake up!" he commands.

The senses of his second oldest son gradually obey. "It's OK." Bill pours forth reassurances, holding him as panic-stricken gasps give way to calm breaths.

For Bill, the ability to clutch his arms around his frantic boy's trembling shoulder blades is relished, if bittersweet. For 10 years, Bill spent "every waking moment" working to free his son from what he calls an "injustice system" that held him in the prisons of two different states for the crime of drug addiction in 21st-century America. In the process, he drained his already dwindling savings, flying from state to state as Colorado and Washington played ping-pong with DOC#832037.

He was allowed to hug Nathan for only seven seconds whenever he'd visit him at Washington State Penitentiary in Walla Walla, Nathan's home for 33 months until this past spring.

He acted as Nathan's de facto lawyer when he thought his son's defense attorneys weren't doing enough. He met with senators, prosecutors, attorneys general, activists—anyone who could do something to free Nathan, among the millions incarcerated for simple drug possession in the United States.

Bill believed that his son should receive treatment, not prison, for his two-decade drug dependency.

Nathan did make it out. And for a time Bill had his son back. However, old demons resurfaced. Nathan would again be torn from his grasp.

As Bill Austin sits in the conference room of the Hillman City Collaboratory in late October sharing barbecued baked beans and potato salad with his partner Diane Whitman, he smiles.

Slim, trim, and bald, his 6'3" athletic frame more than hints at glory days of college-basketball stardom in his hometown of Milwaukee, Wisconsin. and on-court battles against his friend, Seattle Supersonics legend, and godfather to Nathan, Slick Watts.

Today he's reminiscing about his son's childhood days in Redmond—better days, when Nathan was a straight-A honor student at The Overlake School scoring in the 90th percentile nationally on standardized tests. Then everything changed.

"He was almost beaten to death," Bill says, pushing baked beans around his paper plate.

Nathan lays out the tale of the day his childhood ended in a letter to supporters, written while in prison in Walla Walla.

A promising basketball star who had inherited his father's talent on the hardwood, Nathan was preparing for his first season of high-school basketball, where he would play alongside Watts' son. Though a freshman, the tall, lanky athlete was likely to start on the varsity team.

While walking home from a movie theater on Halloween night, he was mistaken by gang members for the son of a rival Mexican gang leader, according to Bill. They beat him with golf clubs, stomped his head so hard that they broke Nathan's orbital bone, and fractured his skull. They finished by stabbing him in the stomach with a screwdriver. Pummeled almost beyond recognition and covered in blood, Nathan was thrown into a ditch and left to die.

Doctors assessed Nathan as most likely suffering brain damage. Several follow-up appointments were scheduled after his initial rehabilitation, but the teen never showed up for any.

Nathan would sob uncontrollably to the point of vomiting when he was alone, his father said. In his letter, Nathan describes fears that he would be seen as an outcast by his high-school classmates.

Why can't he stop the images flashing in his head of blood dirtying the air as fists rush his face? Why does his stomach knot up anytime he's around others, including his family? Why can't he stop crying?

Once outgoing, he started to turn inward. Soon he started drinking; harder drugs followed.

The depression would flood back whenever he wasn't using, Nathan writes. In his letter, Nathan confesses to feeling responsible for being beaten, responsible for his parents' divorce senior year of high school, responsible for anything that went wrong.

Years passed. Nathan managed to don a smile in public at work every day, but couldn't keep a job past a few months. The depression would become too severe, and he'd suddenly quit and go on a drug bender.

His mother moved to Grand Junction, Colorado, after divorcing Bill, and both parents thought it would be a great place for Nathan to reset his life. It was, for a little while. In 2002, at age 24, he started classes at Mesa State College. He excelled in his studies.

However, depression followed him. To battle it this time, he used Adderall, a prescription drug meant to treat attention deficit disorder and said to offer a boost similar to that of cocaine. But then he was introduced to a newer, cheaper drug as plentiful on his college campus as Skittles are on middle-school playgrounds: methamphetamine.

Six months later he faced his first possession charge. Less than a month after that, he was charged a second time for the same offense.

A month later, lost in addiction's abyss and under arraignment for his second drug possession, he chose not to dispose of the drugs he'd stolen from a dealer the previous night. While he was being arraigned, officers found two ounces on him, enough for Mesa County prosecutors to hang a charge of "possession with the intent to distribute" on him.

Facing a possible 12-year sentence, he agreed to a plea deal. Five years in prison.

That was the first time he said goodbye to his then-wife and 6-month-old daughter. He had no possibility of parole and a mandatory release date of August 25, 2008. He was sent to Sterling Correctional Facility, on the eastern plains of Colorado.

During those five years, the serial drug abuser was forced to share a cell with a murderer, and then a rapist. There was never a night without fear, according to Nathan's letter.

It was in December 2009, just a little over a year after getting out of Sterling, when Nathan had another run-in with the police. During a traffic stop outside Grand Junction, Mesa County officers discovered a sandwich bag containing trace amounts of meth in the backseat cushion of the car he was riding in. Nathan was arrested and locked up in the local jail.

Nathan, who is black, told the arresting officers the bag wasn't his. The officers handcuffed him anyway, while allowing the driver and the car's other passenger, both white, to go free.

It was Nathan's fourth arrest for drug possession in the past seven years, meaning that if he were found guilty, the state of Colorado could impose a 24-year mandatory minimum sentence under a Habitual Criminal Charge. It would be Nathan's second extended drug sentence, after the recent five-year stint at Sterling.

A week later, writing from a Mesa County Jail cell, Nathan drafted a plea to Judge Thomas Deister. In it, Nathan admitted to using drugs for the past 18 years, during which he'd tried to break free of his addiction, but relapsed after a tumultuous period in his life that included chronic bouts of severe depression and a divorce (he'd become estranged from his wife the year before). In his letter, he maintained that the empty sandwich bag found in the car was not his while admitting that he needed help with his addiction. In his nearly two decades of drug use, he had never stepped foot inside a rehab center.

Nathan wrote that he wanted to be placed inside a recently opened 90-day in-patient program called the Summit View Program in Grand Junction.

Deister never responded to his request, while the prosecution viewed treatment as a non-starter, offering Nathan a lesser sentence of six years behind bars if, and only if, he pled guilty.

Nathan says he initiated contact with Mesa's Transitional Coordinator, Marivel McClelland, to apply for inpatient treatment himself. She said she would be able to procure Nathan a bed, and lined up employment and shared housing upon successful completion of the rehab program. Meanwhile, his parole officer recommended his charge be reduced to petty paraphernalia.

His father used $10,000 of his savings on defense attorney Jon Levine, with the hope that Levine could reach an agreement with prosecution that would allow Nathan to avoid incarceration. Awaiting trial, Nathan spent 18 months alone in a gray-walled cell in county jail. During those months, Nathan volunteered for every substance-abuse and life-enrichment class Mesa offered. He completed nine courses, and even had a role in the creation of a faith-based drug-recovery group.

Despite his personal progress, his work with other inmates in the prison, and his work to develop a comprehensive action plan upon his release, the prosecution refused to entertain an in-patient treatment plan. The best Levine could do was the exact bargain Nathan had been offered all those months ago: plead guilty to felony possession of a controlled substance and serve six years in prison.

As Nathan's trial date drew near, the prosecution tacked on the Habitual Criminal Charge against him—which the Austins claim the prosecution had promised not to do. Judge Diester granted the new charge, which meant that Nathan now faced two decades in prison unless he took the plea deal.

The original letter Nathan wrote to Diester asking to be placed in a treatment facility was admitted into evidence by the prosecution as an admission of Nathan's guilt.

Both of the two un-arrested, un-jailed people who were in the car with Nathan the fateful night he was arrested agreed to testify against him.

Outraged, Bill demanded and received a sit-down with Mesa County District Attorney Pete Hautzinger. Bill arrived at Hautzinger's office with a drug-addiction specialist, Nathan's parole officer, and an attorney in tow. He pleaded for drug treatment for Nathan.

There was some hope. Hautzinger served on the Comprehensive Sentencing Task Force for Colorado's Commission on Criminal and Juvenile Justice, formed in 2007, which at the time was on the verge of doing away with stiff sentences for drug offenders. However, those changes wouldn't have applied to Nathan, who was facing a fifth charge. And Hautzinger insisted Nathan's case had been handled appropriately.

Nathan pled guilty to felony possession. Diester heaped another 16 years of felony probation on top of the 6 year sentence, along with 1,600 hours of community service, and $12,000 in fines and fees.

Nathan did eventually receive some leniency. After serving only part of his six-year sentence, he was released. He moved home, arriving in Seattle on New Year's Eve 2011 to live with his father and his daughter, whom Nathan had barely seen since she was 6 months old.

Adapting to a world he'd been absent from for years was tough. Nathan was plagued by nightmares of rotting alone in a colorless Colorado cell, time gnawing away at his body.

In his waking hours, employment proved difficult to find. The Seattle City Council would eventually pass an ordinance preventing employers from rejecting the applications of convicted felons outright, but not in time for Nathan. He found it impossible to get work.

Depression started slowly to consume him. The outside world was as unforgiving as the system that took him from it for a time. He tried hard in those first 10 months of freedom to resist the urge to use, but the temptation became unbearable as hard luck again found him.

On November 3, 2012, Nathan was scheduled to check in with his parole officer. In his letter, Nathan claimed that he hadn't realized that—that he'd thought his PO had changed the meeting to mid-November. A phone call informed him that, whether through a filing error or a miscommunication, he was mistaken.

He says the parole officer informed him, "There's now a warrant out for your arrest."

And so Nathan ran, parking his body on the frigid pavement of Thurston County's streets during a harsh winter.

Hungry, fearful, and suicidal, he again turned to drugs to tame his depression. He stole a car, parking it in the woods near Tumwater as a temporary shelter from freezing winds and chilling rain.

On February 28, 2013, Nathan was arrested for vehicle theft and sent to Walla Walla. There he was diagnosed with attention deficit hyperactivity disorder and post-traumatic stress disorder, stemming from his childhood attack, Nathan writes. Those diagnoses led to him being properly medicated; with his disorders under control, he was accepted into the state's Drug Offender Sentencing Alternative treatment program, and signed up for classes through Walla Walla Community College. He excelled in Graphic Design; his first-quarter grades yielded a GPA of 3.7.

On good behavior, he was accepted into the Rap House/Lincoln Park Work release program in Tacoma. The program, which treats co-occurring disorders, such as his PTSD and drug addiction, would put him closer to his family and the support it offered. Things were looking up for the 37-year-old.

Then Colorado came calling again.

Nathan's arrest in Washington meant a violation of his 16-year probation, stemming back to that empty baggie. Mesa County District Court placed an extradition warrant on him, and planned to extract him as soon as his Washington sentence was up, removing him from his work-release program and his family, guaranteeing that he will not be free from the Colorado Department of Corrections until his mid-50s.

Bill kept fighting, enduring sleepless nights as he challenged the extradition order. He knocked on the doors of anyone he thought could help, from Governor Jay Inslee to Senator Maria Cantwell. Bill says he even persuaded Secret Service personnel to deliver a letter to Attorney General Loretta Lynch when she visited Seattle.

The argument was sound in Bill's mind. Nathan had gotten his life together while in Walla Walla; what unforgivable debt does he owe society? Why burden taxpayers with the incarceration of a nonviolent offender?

Whom did he harm, other than himself and his own family?

"It makes zero sense to lock a drug addict up," says Lance Dodes, a former Harvard Medical School professor whose work details the "bad science" behind our country's understanding of addiction and the failures of its rehabilitation methods.

"Addiction is a psychological thing," he says over the phone from his Beverly Hills home. "It is a compulsion like overeating or rearranging things on a desk. No one wants to criminalize someone for compulsive overeating, but we do so with drug addicts."

The author of three books on alternative drug treatments, Dodes has two problems with the way America treats addicts. First, that it miscategorizes drug abuse as a "brain disease," based on a disputed study of rats and heroin by the National Institute of Drug Abuse, rather than a compulsive disorder. The other is its inability to distinguish the glaring difference between criminals and addicts.

Of the 1,488,707 Americans arrested for drug-law violations in 2015 alone, 16.1 percent were for the sale or manufacture of drugs. The other 83.9 percent were for simple possession.

"Those benefiting from selling the substance should be treated as criminals, those who have the compulsion should be treated," Dodes says. "That's not hard to distinguish." He believes the main culprit of drug addicts' continued criminalization is our nation's embedded puritanical view of drug use as immoral and weak.

About 20.1 million Americans suffered from a drug disorder last year, says Dodes, pointing out that good treatment options are rarely available for them.

Peer-reviewed data shows that programs like Alcoholics Anonymous rarely work, with a success rate between 5 and 10 percent. Most people don't understand that a person has peaks and valleys in recovering from addiction, he says, which include tolerating the occasional relapse. "Would you expect a compulsive eater to never overeat again?" he asks. In the case of Nathan and addicts like him, Dodes suggests serious psychotherapy that would address the root causes of his addiction, namely his attack when he was 14 years old.

An avid reader of Dodes' work and a former drug and alcohol counselor himself, Bill Austin knew his son desperately needed such treatment.

Bill effectively quit work at his car dealership, stopped coaching youth basketball, and rarely took any social engagements. He wrote nearly every one of the nation's 100 senators to detail Nathan's plight; tried to find allies in the prison-abolitionist movement that had gained traction after Michelle Alexander's book *The New Jim Crow* brought attention to America's mass-incarceration problem; and attended every community meeting he could find looking for sympathetic souls, spending nearly $100,000 on Nathan while he was in prison.

"Bill loves his son unconditionally, and it showed in how hard the man worked to get him released," says Afam Ayika, a community organizer who counseled Bill more than 30 different times over the past two and a half years. "Imagine incarcerated addicts who don't have someone like him fighting for them."

Despite his efforts, it appeared that Nathan would soon be the property of Colorado's Department of Corrections. Unless a miracle happened.

That miracle arrived in the form of an odd coupling of a maverick City Attorney from Seattle who once instructed his subordinates to not prosecute marijuana smokers prior to legalization, and a straight-laced Assistant District Attorney in one of Colorado's most conservative bastions.

"Bill is the persistent widow," Seattle City Attorney Pete Holmes says from his Columbia Tower office on a recent afternoon, referring to the Biblical tale of a widow who pesters an unmoving judge until he delivers her justice. Bill, sitting next to Holmes, chuckles at the comparison.

Bill and Holmes have a history together, but it took a while for Nathan's plight to reach the City Attorney's attention. When Holmes learned of Nathan's situation, he stepped in. "This was something I thought could be handled prosecutor to prosecutor," he says. In search of a resolution, he reached out to Richard Tuttle, the Assistant District Attorney in Mesa County overseeing Nathan's extradition.

Over five months, beginning in November 2015, Holmes had seven separate calls with Tuttle regarding Nathan. Holmes informed Tuttle that Nathan could be accepted into the Tacoma outpatient treatment program only if Colorado's extradition warrant was retracted.

Seeing no reason to deprive a drug addict from that support group—and noting that Nathan's mother no longer lived in Colorado—Tuttle petitioned the court to quash Nathan's warrant on March 14 of this year. The next day Mesa County dropped the extradition claim.

On June 2 Nathan came home.

Bill's high-wattage smile resurfaces when he thinks of the day Nathan walked through the front door, hugging his siblings and snapping photos that were soon posted on social media. Nathan's daughter, now a teenager, had tears pouring from her face as her father held her.

The last time Nathan's family saw him was on Father's Day. His daughter had come by Bill's house to spend time with her father. He said he needed to take off for a moment but would be back.

He never returned.

Bill suspected this might happen. He had begged his son's community corrections officer in the outpatient Tacoma program to place him in an in-patient program where he would receive counseling for his mental disorder. Without it, Nathan's re-entry into society would be fraught and, Bill knew too well, temporary.

"I told Nathan's CCO that I'd been trying to get him treatment for six years," Bill says now. "He's not just going to walk into treatment. He's got mental disorders along with his drug thing." Bill explains that Nathan was not given mandatory inpatient treatment as his son had requested. Instead the CCO would "tell him" to check himself into treatment should he relapse.

Still, Bill won't quit—if not for Nathan, then to change the criminal-justice system he feels failed his son.

There has been some hope. While harder drugs have yet to seriously be considered, seven states have currently decriminalized marijuana, and a national conversation has been spurred around drug reform with America's current opioid epidemic, killing 27,000 people a year.

Bill says the latter has gotten attention only because drugs have finally started ravaging white households on a vast scale, as they have black communities for decades. However, he'll take the concern any way he can get it.

There is also Seattle's Law Enforcement Assisted Diversion program, which diverts drug offenders from one prosecution if they agree to work with a case manager to find employment and counseling. The program has become a model for other municipalities.

All this is cold consolation to Bill, however, as he prepares to again deal with the criminal-justice system when Nathan eventually returns to him. If he returns.

In the ensuing months, Nathan's six siblings have mostly given up on their brother. They've seen the toll Bill's fight has taken on him: high stress levels, a lack of financial security in old age. "Most of them don't understand why he keeps going back to drugs," Bill says.

And as for Nathan's daughter?

"She doesn't really want anything to do with her father right now," he confesses.

After all he's sacrificed over the years, why can't Bill quit?

"Because he's my son."

El Centro de la Raza Offers Lessons for Community Land Use

by Will Sweger

Sitting in the office of El Centro de la Raza, surrounded by colorful murals and creaking wooden floors, you would not guess you are in the epicenter of a modern apartment complex. In reality, though, it is the heart of something more—an alternative model for urban living.

The North Beacon Hill landmark is home to almost 300 people of every race and hosts on-site after-school programs for local youths. Plaza Roberto Maestas, named after the founder of El Centro de la Raza, is a public gathering space decorated with vibrant tiles arrayed by local artists. The new buildings bordering the plaza offer space to several small businesses including the Station café and a newly arrived Tacos Chukis shop. The community even hosts movie screenings in the summer.

Part of what makes the location special is that it is one of the few places in the city offering low-income housing sized for families and maintains a community-centered applicant selection process. Understandably, the demand is high, hearkening back to the site's opening in the winter of 2016 that saw hundreds of people standing in line for a chance to rent a home here.

Estela Ortega, Executive Director of El Centro de la Raza and partner of the late founder Roberto Maestas, was animated as she discussed the expansion, occasionally rapping on the table for emphasis. After the success of the new buildings, she said churches and other organizations regularly ask how to follow El Centro de la Raza's example for community land use.

Protest Action

The protest action that led to El Centro began in 1972, four years after the assassination of Martin Luther King Jr. and just two years after the Ohio State National Guard fired on a group of protesters killing four students. Indigenous rights groups had just ended their occupations of Alcatraz Island in San Francisco and Fort Lawton in Seattle. The promise of Lyndon Johnson's Great Society had broken down as the war in Vietnam drew more attention and funding.

Roberto Maestas, an activist and organizer, was teaching English as a second language courses at South Seattle Community College when the state cut funding for the program motivating Maestas, his students and fellow teachers and community activists to take action. They peaceably occupied the abandoned Beacon Hill School and, later, the office of then Seattle Mayor Wes Uhlman. The demonstration led to an agreement to lease the property to Roberto Maestas for the symbolic sum of one dollar a year. Maestas founded El Centro de la Raza as a community-focused non-profit on the property.

Though the protest focused on Latino rights, other members of communities of color, the faith community, and anti-war activists joined the occupiers. The occupation itself provided housing for several community members through the Seattle winter.

Explaining the financial hardship the organization faced in the 70s and 80s, Ortega said, "we felt like we were always fighting for everything, occupying offices and picketing to demand resources for our community."

"Our time came when the City of Seattle decided to put a light rail station here on Beacon Hill," Ortega explained. El Centro de la Raza would now sit on a busy, pedestrian-friendly transportation hub. The non-profit worked to buy the property and plan for a capital campaign to raise money to build low-income family-sized housing. In 1999, they bought the land from the city for about 1.2 million dollars and began renovating the site.

GRASSROOTS ORGANIZING

Ortega said the city sent a representative to conduct a public meeting for input, but failed to complete the networking leg-work necessary to ensure a turnout. As a result, the event flopped. "As a community-based organization you can never give up your organizing to anybody," Ortega explained.

Explaining the process, she said, "we had our vision of what we wanted to happen out here so based on that vision, we organized. We organized people who had never participated in a process like this." Organizers met at separate meetings and organized who would speak at public gatherings in favor of including child care facilities, low-income housing units, a park, and other amenities in the new development.

Ortega recalled over 30 public meetings where community members came together to reach a consensus about how to shape their neighborhood. "You absolutely have to involve the community in the process," she explained.

Originally from Baja, California, Luis Rodriguez, the co-owner of the Station coffee shop, said he had not heard of a community centered non-profit before he encountered El Centro de la Raza. He said organizers from El Centro approached him to invite him to community land development discussions. "I was very happy to be a part of those meetings because I had an input in finding out what was going to be the use for this land."

Administrative Infrastructure

Prior to expanding into providing housing on its main lot, El Centro's staff cut their teeth administering several housing arrangements. Describing them as "transitional housing," Ortega said El Centro purchased two houses in the 1980s to help ease the local homeless problem. Eventually, the non-profit began to manage a 14-unit apartment building two blocks away. Providing housing management allowed the staff to gain experience with financial audits, record keeping, office technology, and a better understanding of the legal landscape.

Describing the fundraising phase of building affordable housing, Ortega said El Centro de la Raza had a devoted capital campaign director and a grant writer, but "When we have things that are big, the entire organization is involved in one way or another. We don't just leave it to one department to have it as their sole responsibility because if you do it's not going to work."

With proper administration, Ortega said up-and-coming non-profits who have land and a commitment "can develop housing in their respective communities and not have to have somebody, because they have resources, to own part of their project."

TIME

With pain in her eyes, Ortega described the seven and a half years it took to raise money and complete the project. She said community members began to fear they wouldn't build anything.

Non-profit housing projects take a longer time to complete because they require organizers to juggle all aspects of the endeavor, including fundraising, design approval, and construction. With $47 million going towards paying for the new construction and supporting infrastructure, raising the money slowed the process substantially.

To complete the project, the staff of El Centro de la Raza combined state funding, grants, a $5 million loan, and individual donations over five and a half years. "The hard work in [fundraising] is that you have to know people who have money." Ortega explained. "That's tough."

DEDICATION TO COMMUNITY

Throughout the process, Ortega said the leadership of El Centro turned down offers of development for market-rate housing, studio apartments, and one bedrooms in favor of low-income units with the capacity for small families. "There was big money involved," Ortega said. "They wanted to own a part of your project."

Yet, she continued, "El Centro has always been about our own self-determination and we're not going to have somebody own part of something that we have struggled for years and years to maintain."

She said, "…the model shouldn't be having some other entity own part of your property to do a development. We've got to come up with better solutions to help communities develop housing and other types of capital assets."

Though El Centro de la Raza does use a management company for the homes it owns, Ortega said the non-profit maintains the final word on which housing applicants are accepted. Ortega explained that this essential distinction allows El Centro to provide housing for immigrants and people with criminal records.

"Doing this development out here," she said, gesturing south toward new homes and business spaces, "is a night and day change of how the broader community saw El Centro de la Raza."

Looking to the future, Ortega expressed a fear that funding for social programming will once again be cut, mirroring the conditions that led to the occupation in the 70s. To weather the storm, El Centro is planning to move towards more independent revenue streams to avoid depending on loans, grants, and fundraising.

For small business owners, however, the present is paying off. Rodriguez said his business almost tripled after moving across the street into the new complex next to the light rail station. He praised the large, street-level windows since they allow him to see the busy intersection as he works the counter and they allow the community to see him.

"Hopefully they can build more places like this. Hopefully this building can become the example for other neighborhoods," Rodriguez said. "We don't have to build these condos and those apartments and push people out so we can squeeze every single penny from people, but instead build community with one building."

ONE MUSLIM AMERICAN VETERAN VOICES HER STRENGTH, FEARLESSNESS DESPITE UNCERTAIN FUTURE

by Kelsey Hamlin

Mujaahidah Sayfullah is an American Muslim and a U.S. Army combat veteran from Tacoma, Washington. She served for six years, including in Operation Desert Storm.

While many people find themselves shaken by despair and fear as a result of an impending Donald Trump presidency, Sayfullah remains optimistic.

"I'm just a strong, individual woman, and it's hard for me to see everyone so sad," she said. "I want good for all of mankind, even Trump."

Sayfullah is well-informed about how the election process works, and had been watching the polls come in throughout the day on Tuesday. When Trump gained over 270 electoral college votes, she said she wasn't surprised, although she admitted to being taken aback a little bit.

"Anything is possible when people are misinformed about the election voting process," Sayfullah said. "I think people are unaware of how the electoral votes are really what matters, so I think people underestimated the electoral sway with Trump."

She argued that Trump's platform was honest, and although she called it "ridiculous" and "obnoxious," the Muslim American vet felt his honesty was what made people so attracted to his platform.

Being a Muslim American is one identity, being a veteran is another, so is being a woman, and so is being a person of color. Sayfullah sits at the intersection of all these identities, embodying them simultaneously.

"So I have these obstacles to face every day I walk out that door," she said. Typically, Sayfullah goes to the Veteran Affairs Hospital for medical services. "I often get stared at. I do. Like I don't belong there, like, 'how dare you be here; you're not part of us; you can't possibly be a veteran; how dare you.'"

On Wednesday, she was doing an interview on Main Street, downtown, when someone honked their horn at her. Sayfullah admitted to not being entirely sure what the intention of the driver was, but she said it hadn't happened before.

"It's just sad that it still goes on after 9/11," she said, referring to the day the twin towers were struck by hijacked airplanes, which ultimately led to a change in American rhetoric, security, and war.

Walking around, however, Sayfullah did say she noticed a shift in people's behaviors and attitudes toward her.

"I kinda think with Trump being elected, it kind of perpetuated the deep rooted hatred within people," Sayfullah said. "But I'm not afraid. I don't fear any man."

The core of Sayfullah's being is her religion, Islam, and she explained that it is her faith that gives her the ability to feel as unfazed as she does by today's political environment.

"I have to be an example to show what Islam is about," she said. "And Islam is about peace."

Sayfullah defines that example for herself as being positive. While she said she can't believe some of the things Trump has said and done, everyone can be forgiven. But she does have a 12 year-old who was so concerned that he was coming up to her and constantly showing her the polls.

"He was scared," she said. "A lot of Muslim children have the fear they'll be attacked at school or racial slurs will come out."

Regardless, she said her son went to school, and so far everything has been fine. Sayfullah felt that children are scared because they fear the unknown, and they shouldn't have that fear.

"Many girls will take off their hijab because they're afraid of how they'll be treated if they're identified as Muslim," she explained.

The way to battle these types of anxieties for Sayfullah is education. She explained that her son had gone to school to meet many more children who were as anxious and scared as he was on election night, but her son relayed the words of Sayfullah.

"It made me feel good that he could help other children, too, who hadn't had a talk with their parents, and find comfort and ease that everything is going to be alright," she said. "They're worried about the world now because of their future leaders. So it's important to put morals and values in the youth and educate them as well."

There are 3.3 million Muslims in the United States of America. Yes, these Muslims are also American.

"Choosing Life": Cancer Support Group Founder Continues to Enlighten, Educate While Battling Disease

by Reagan Jackson

22 years ago, Bridgette Hempstead had a visit to the doctor that changed her life. What started out as a routine checkup turned into an argument.

"I called my doctor and said I wanted to get a mammogram," Hempstead recounted. "She began to give me a laundry list of reasons why I did not need to get a mammogram and the last reason, which I think is the most disturbing one, is she said I am African American and African Americans don't need to worry about breast cancer."

The doctor suggested that with no history of cancer in her family that Hempstead didn't need the test and should come back in 10 years. Hempstead insisted and was given a mammogram. She was diagnosed with breast cancer on her 35th birthday. Her doctor broke the news and apologized for being dismissive stating she had been taught in medical school that breast cancer was not a disease that impacted African Americans.

"Even during that time that was not a true assessment because even at that time black women were dying at an alarming rate," said Hempstead. "They may not have had the same amount of diagnosis, but the disparities were horrifying. And during that time younger black women were being diagnosed, but they were being late-stage diagnosis because of the symptoms that were being ignored at the time."

Hempstead described the late 90s as a time when the only visual representation associated with breast cancer was white women with pink ribbons. There was a disconnect. What about people of color or black women celebrating life after breast cancer or diagnosis?

"The numbers or the education was not there for black women," explained Hempstead. "That's how I started the Cierra Sisters because there was a huge need and I was in the education system back then so my education skills changed from educating children to educating the women in our community about breast cancer and about surviving the disease and educating yourself so that you can be properly diagnosed and get a proper treatment."

Cierra means knowledge. For the past 22 years Hempstead has dedicated her time and talent towards building the Cierra Sisters into a community of support, education, and advocacy with the hope that in providing better access to knowledge and support, black women could find a pathway forward into better health.

The Cierra Sisters host community meetings on the fourth Thursdays of the month from 6:15-8:15pm at Rainier Beach Community Center. The meetings often feature speakers in different medical professions, but are also an opportunity for survivor to survivor support and information sharing about how to navigate the healthcare system.

"Those meetings are really important. Very informational, very bonding because you've got women that can see other women that are going through similar things that look just like them," said Hempstead. "When you leave that meeting you're leaving empowered, encouraged and ready to deal with whatever you have to deal with when it comes to having cancer. "

These meetings are not only for women. Everyone is welcome, whether they are a survivor or the friend or family member of a survivor or simply want to educate themselves.

In addition to hosting a monthly support group for survivors, the Cierra Sisters host conferences, put on a Wellness festival in the summer, and even go door to door to make sure people in our community are getting the education they need to advocate for themselves.

"I made sure that our community would know what to do based off of my own experience and it's a very personal experience dealing with breast cancer," said Hempstead.

Hempstead, currently a resident of Rainier Beach, grew up in South Sacramento during the era of the Black Panthers. She married young and had three daughters before getting a divorce and moving to Seattle. In addition to her work with the Cierra Sisters she teaches in the Medical Administrative Assistant Program at Seattle Vocational Institute, is a consultant with Fred Hutch and serves on the board of the South Seattle Emerald. Several years ago she began working with renowned oncologist Dr. Julie Gralow to do breast health education in Uganda, Zambia, Rwanda, Tanzania, and soon Kenya.

"In those particular countries disparities are pretty horrifying so part of the educational piece that I do is to teach women about breast health and about their bodies and really looking at the positive in the face of such a horrifying disease that has killed so many women across the world," said Hempstead.

After 18 years of being in remission, Hempstead was diagnosed with Metastatic cancer. She had just returned from Uganda and was having some problems breathing so she went to urgent care. Her initial scans warranted further follow up, but when she tried to schedule a second appointment she was once again met with resistance. Her case had been passed onto a second physician.

"He said just take this cough medicine and you'll be fine. So the next day I get up and I call my doctor and they say there's no follow up, you just need to finish taking the cough medicine and you'll be fine."

After her previous experience, Hempstead did not take no for an answer. She advocated for herself. "Well, the nurse who is on the other end of the line says well I don't see anything and then she got very quiet and then she gasps. She says oh my goodness, the first orders were erased, but you can't totally erase the records. So then she went ahead and followed up so that I could go get a biopsy."

Cancer is scary, but even more terrifying is the realization of how life-threatening racial bias can be when it comes to accessing healthcare as a black woman. A study by the American Cancer Society reports that black women are 39 percent more likely to die from cancer than white women, not because (as some have suggested) black women are attacked with more aggressive forms of cancer, but because their medical concerns are dismissed which leads to later diagnosis.

"I think the most disturbing thing about that for me is how many other people does this happen to?" asks Hempstead. "You need to find out what's going on with you and the earlier the better because of the incredible treatments that are available out there and individuals that find themselves faced with something life threatening, I think its important to try to live a normal life and not allow the health care system that may not have respect for you dictate how you should plan your life."

Upon receiving her most recent diagnosis, Hempstead was told she only had one year left to live. "And I jumped off the table with my daughter in the room and I told that doctor I don't receive that in the name of Jesus and my daughter said let's go."

They booked tickets to Jamaica and went parasailing. When she came back, armed with the knowledge of 18 years of advocacy work, Hempstead selected another doctor to work with who specialized in metastatic cancer and has been receiving excellent treatment.

"You know the bible says tomorrow is not promised, but in that same scripture for Bridgette today is that tomorrow that wasn't promised. So each day we have an opportunity to do the best that we can not only to love ourselves, but to love others as we're dealing with health challenges, as we're dealing with family challenges, as we're dealing with issues surrounding us."

Hempstead plans to continue loving herself and her community through her steadfast commitment to health. She is also contemplating going back to school in order to develop programs for other organizations.

"Nobody is going to get out here without leaving this earth, but it's what you do while you're here," said Hempstead who has lived three and a half years longer than her doctor said she would. "It's how you live your life and what kind of quality of life you have, what kind of human being can you be to another human being. I think that's so important. Instead of contemplating or concentrating on death, how about concentrating on living your best life today."

FREEDOM SCHOOL IMMERSES STUDENTS
IN LIBERATION EDUCATION

by Sharayah Lane

As the year comes to a close and the haze of an election filled with racism, sexism and xenophobia moves closer to an inaugural reality, walking into a Freedom School is no doubt a revitalizing and liberating experience for south Seattle's youth.

Freedom Schools are a bi-annual experience organized by American Friends Service Committee and Youth Undoing Institutional Racism at United Church of Christ on Beacon Hill in South Seattle. They are a space for healing, a space for collective organization, and an immersion into an education that is so often suppressed in our public school systems.

All who enter the space are asked to introduce themselves. Activities are paused to make sure that everyone is acknowledged. "What's your name? What do you do? Why is it urgent to undo racism?" The same three questions are asked of everyone upon arrival. The third question has the power to, when contemplated, thrust anyone into the current state of racial reality in our country.

This afternoon's curriculum focused on the construction of race and its distortion toward Black people from the earliest scientific classifications. Next the group discussed the transition from indentured servitude to race-based slavery. "What would happen to that 1% class if the Native Americans, the slaves of African descent, and the poor Europeans were to work together?" asked a facilitator. This question was followed up by a call to "raise your hand if you've ever heard of the Black Codes."

What is race? What are the benefits of enacting a law that says an enslaved woman's children are enslaved automatically? What is a social construct? These were just a few questions posed to students. One student gives her definition of a social construct while another follows up with a reminder that deeming race a social construct often undermines the true extent of the destruction it wields.

These students know their stuff and have come to learn more.

"We are trying to push young people to a new level of consciousness with the end goal of giving them the tools for organizing and taking action," said program coordinator Senait Brown. "The Freedom School is based on popular education and the curriculum is largely shaped by who is in the room. What we discuss is always based around what folks are experiencing now."

Freedom Schools started in Mississippi during the summer of 1964 as a coordinated effort by the Student Nonviolent Coordinating Committee to register Blacks to vote. The schools were an opportunity for all people in the Black community to get an opportunity to learn about things such as Black history and African culture. It wasn't uncommon for students to attend who were in their 50s and 60s.

South Seattle's Freedom School, founded by Dustin Washington, is designed for students age 15 – 23, but anyone at any age is invited to participate. No one is turned away. The power of social media allows some of our youngest citizens to know all too well the weight of racism in America. Children often look to their families and teachers for answers to tough questions about race and equity. 11-year-old Myanna got to add the Freedom School to her arsenal of knowledge on herself and her Blackness. Her grandma told her about the school and she learned within her own life why it was important for her to get the education.

"When I was younger I used to be really, really scared of Black people, I was scared because of what people were telling me at my school. I was scared of my own family sometimes, but I would always go to white people. I would always think that they were the ones who were going to be there. Then my grandma showed me why this was wrong, she taught me the history of racism," said Myanna, "then I came to Freedom School and started learning what really happened. Before I didn't really care for black people and then I learned that I'm black, these are my people and we all stand together in this nation as one."

For other participants the Freedom School has become a space of healing; healing for themselves and, in turn, their families. 23-year-old Robert

Gavino, a first generation Filipino American, is attending his second Freedom School in the company of friends he insisted needed to experience the power of the education.

"I consider this experience very healing and being able to bring more of my family, friends and community into this healing is one reason I came back to the Freedom School for a second time," said Gavino. "If any of us wants to live full meaningful lives we have to bring each other along in this education and deeper understanding,"

And with the seemingly endless imagery of black and brown bodies subjugated to destruction and the elusive silhouette of justice throughout 2016 and previous years, the Freedom School atop Beacon Hill is an enlightened haven of collaboration, education, hope and most of all, freedom.

Crediting Fitness With Saving His Life, World Champion Power-lifter Uses It to Aid Seniors

by Marcus Harrison Green

It's just five minutes past 10:00 on a sunny Friday morning in the Southeast Seattle Senior Center's (SESSC) recreation room, and exercise coach Mark Bryant will be damned if he allows his fitness class an easy path into the weekend. Over acid rock-tinged background music, he barks forceful commands to a dozen sitting seniors. They obey, rolling their neck in a circular motion to the right, then the left, then curling their torsos under their feet, then hovering their fingers over their toes.

Between orders, Bryant walks the circle of 60- to late 80-something students and delivers a personalized joke as collegial as his instructions are authoritative. "I see you made sure to bring an outfit that coordinated with your weights," he tells one woman wearing a purple tracksuit that matches her five-pound dumbbells.

After a brief round of small talk, Bryant ratchets up the intensity with an exhaustive circuit of side-to-side toe tapping—what looks like skiing in place—and some arm circles. Though the class has barely lasted a half hour, it looks like it's taken something out of the teacher.

"I've worked so long at this senior center that I'm now a senior myself," laughs the 58-year-old whose chiseled frame resembles Homer's description of Achilles in the Iliad. Bryant has taught here for 12 years, and Friday's class is just one of eight he leads during the week in the South End. His combined pay adds up to "enough to tell a bill collector I'll give you the rest later," he says, but what he lacks in financial gain, he more than makes up for in gratitude from his students.

"I love his sense of humor," says AJ Lowe, who attends both the Friday class at the center and another that Bryant teaches at her apartment complex.

"I've given up on other exercise programs. He gives me hope that my life isn't over."

As serious and direct as Bryant can come across to those unfamiliar with him (attributes gained from his New York upbringing, he says), it's his ability to inspire laughter in the middle of extreme exercise that has endeared him to his students.

"Mark knows a lot about human beings and our bodies. And he always keeps it fun," says Jeff Panciern, speaking during a five-minute break in the class. "He once had us doing all this choreography. I said, 'With moves like that you have to take us to the disco.'"

This mix of stand-up comic and hardline drill sergeant wasn't always as appreciated as it is now, says Lynda Greene, Executive Director of the SES-SC. "When I first started here eight years ago, I was like, 'He's talking to these people so rough,'" she says. Now, she couldn't imagine anyone else in his role. In fact, neither can his students.

"If we have to have a substitute because he can't make it, students won't come," Greene exclaims. "People light up when they see him. You can't copy someone's personality."

Now a five-time powerlifting champion, Bryant brings more than just good humor to the group. He has a deep knowledge of human physiology, which his students credit with helping them battle physical impediments they long accepted as part of everyday life.

"I've gone to so many so-called trainers who weren't able to give me valid advice," recounts Matthew Jones. That wasn't so with Bryant, who Jones first met 7 years ago at the gym when he was attempting a return to power lifting after a debilitating injury. "Mark was able to explain what muscles were being impacting when I'd lift and which ones weren't. When you're older you have to train differently. He convinced me this was the guy I wanted to train with, and he inspired me to start competing again."

Bryant's students often use the word "genius" when describing his vast knowledge of the human body—information cultivated over years of study and practice. On the wall of the center's office space, the instructor proudly displays his latest certificate: a National Commission for Certifying Agencies accreditation in personal training, which is the equivalent of evidence of a lawyer having passed the Bar exam.

With his knowledge, charisma, and magnetic personality, it's easy to wonder why he's leading classes at senior centers, Good Wills, and assisted living complexes rather than high-end gyms. "I've worked at the [Washington Athletic Club] and other places. Those places aren't for brothers," he says. "I'll just be a straight-up New Yorker with you."

He says it's about helping those in need, regardless of whether they can afford to pay. Most of his South End clientele cannot.

"Look, I'm gonna help someone who needs it. If they can pay, great, if they can't, then they can't. But I'm going to try and help someone regardless," Bryant says, adding that most trainers at gym franchises are more concerned with pay than a client's health.

His approach has paid off for him, at least once in a big way. Five years ago, an orthopedic surgeon read an article about a lingering hip problem plaguing Bryant. Admiring the personal trainer's selflessness, the surgeon offered his services for free. After years of suffering Bryant was finally relieved of chronic pain.

In addition to instructing seniors, Bryant also teaches a free boxing class to teenagers, and writes an unpaid fitness column geared toward seniors for Prime Time Northwest.

His compulsion to help was forged during his New York upbringing, which Bryant describes as brutal.

He shares stories of a decade of physical abuse that he and his mother suffered at the hands of his paratrooper stepfather. "He was an alcoholic 7 days a week, and, of course, when he drank it just made him crazy," Bryant says of the man who beat him so badly as an 11-year-old that Bryant almost died. For his mother, the abuse resulted in frequent hospital stays. She now lives in Georgia and suffers from seizures and memory problems that Bryant believes are a result of the beatings.

These interactions with his stepfather inspired Bryant to begin lifting weights and practicing martial arts, specifically Gung-Fu. Though boosting his confidence, it failed to provide him with direction. For him, it wasn't enough to simply survive in Queens, he desired to thrive.

"I'm sitting outside one day and wondering what choices do I have? I live in a neighborhood that's real bad and poor and our education system is so-so. But I'm on this stoop thinking this little circle I live in can't be the whole world," he remembers. He asked friends about other cities, and one suggested visiting Seattle. "I knew about as much about Seattle as I did Timbuktu, but I knew it was different from New York," he says.

In 1985, he officially traded the Big Apple for the Emerald City, and hasn't looked back since. Today he lives in Columbia City. "The only thing different from the two cities is that New Yorkers are more direct, otherwise at this point I call myself a Seattleite," he says.

Although the 206 has softened him a bit, he says he does miss the rapid flux of East Coast cities. "People used to say hello to you when you walk down the street. Those are the ones you can tell have been here for awhile. New people are more standoffish," he says about his adopted city, adding that he hopes to never leave it.

It's the city to which he brought back his fifth power-lifting championship (in the 50-year-old age bracket) two weeks ago from the World Championships of Powerlifting held in Las Vegas. Never one to be confused for humble, he says he knew he had already won it before he got on the plane.

As we wrap up our conversation, a student asks if he'll be teaching the next class on Tuesday.

He'll be there. Count on it.

In Times Like These Poets Have to Poet

by Brian Bergen-Aurand

Throughout the day on Thursday, poet and teacher Terrance Hayes gave a series of talks on the campus of Bellevue College. His topic was "Social Justice for Black Lives," and he addressed it through a morning presentation before faculty, students, and staff; a later question and answer session moderated by English professors Nan Ma and Fernando Pérez; and finally at an evening lecture open to the community.

Hayes may be best known for his work *Lighthead*, which won the 2010 National Book Award and was a finalist for the National Book Critics Circle Award. He is also the author of three other books of poetry—*Muscular Music* (1999), *Hip Logic* (2002), and *Wind in a Box* (2006)—and has won numerous recognitions, including a National Endowment for the Arts Fellowship, a Guggenheim Fellowship, and a MacArthur Fellowship.

His latest collection of poetry, *How to be Drawn* (2015), won the National Book Award and has received significant critical acclaim for its uncategorical style and daring engagement with seeing and being seen. According to the back cover, "How, this dynamic collection asks, is the self drawn by and to the paradoxes of the mind, body, and soul; how do we resist being withdrawn, erased?"

In one of my favorite poems from the collection, "How to Draw an Invisible Man," Hayes focuses on living transparently, not invisibly:

... the waterlogged monologues
one who is unseen speaks burst suddenly
from Ralph Ellison's body and because I mean to live
transparently, I am here, bear with me,
describing the contents: ...

This dynamic between being invisible and being transparent would remain a topic of conversation throughout the day. The goal of his work is to evoke "a refined transparency" in response to this tension, Hayes would explain in the afternoon.

Hayes began the morning event appearing on stage in a black tee shirt with the word "FREEDOM" in faded, grey letters printed across the front. He also wore two watches, one on each wrist, something he has done for the past ten years. He opened with a poem from his first book, a move he said was provoked by a conversation he had earlier in the morning—a morning, he acknowledged later, that put him in an angry mood. This mood, he asserted, had energized him for the day's events.

After the first poem, Hayes began reading from a new series of sonnets, ones he was still revising, he said. They were all entitled "American Sonnet for My Past and Future Assassin" and are in response to events that have followed the 2016 Presidential election—the one that put "the Trumpet" (one of Hayes' names for President Donald Trump) into office. As he read through the sonnets for the next twenty-five minutes, Hayes gave little commentary.

He mentioned that he likes to keep it all in the poems themselves. For example, one poem comments on his relation to Langston Hughes and Sylvia Plath. He knows, he says, as a Black poet, he should lean more toward the former writer, but, honestly, he feels pulled closer to the latter. "The Negro Speaks of Rivers" resonates with him, yes, but more of what Plath was doing shows up in his work.

Hayes read a series of 8 to 10 sonnets. (I lost count, perhaps because they all have the same title.) In that small series, he displayed a significant breadth of voice and a complicated layering of themes and ideas that demonstrate why readers have reacted so favorably to his work. He is serious, driven, and fully engaged with the moment. More than other authors I have read of late, Hayes writes as a poet in his time. He is a poet who wears two watches, after all. He is a poet who admits he is obsessed with time, who tells us he writes in the here and now and urges us to live with an awareness of the moment we inhabit. And, all the while, his focus on the body and his sense of humor return to alter that moment, to make it recognizable and then strange—as all good poets should.

This alteration, or "volta" as he described it, is the turn in poetry (especially sonnets) that takes the image and alters our perspective, makes us look at it anew. A sonnet is like a cube, it has six sides, and the poet should keep turning it, Hayes explained. The poem establishes an expectation, responds in a way that shifts that expectation, and in the process alters the expectation with which the reader or listener began. His poem beginning with Hughes and ending with Plath demonstrates this well. So does "American Sonnet for Wanda C." in *How to be Drawn*, where the lover in the poem announces his desire to be "her son," shifting the significance of everything that came before and changing what a son's love might mean.

After he finished reading, Hayes took questions and comments from the audience for twenty minutes. Following a break for lunch, he returned to address questions from the moderators and the audience for another hour. As he discussed the volta in both sessions and as I reread portions of *How to be Drawn* during the break, I saw how this turn works throughout his writing and how it applies to what he calls "poetry of palpable politics" and "the poetics of politics."

The target in Hayes' sonnets and the poems in *How to be Drawn* is the embodied experience of the political moment, not the disembodied ideology of politics in general. He is drawing out the moment of experience in all its carnal, corporeal layers to turn invisible bodies into transparent ones. He writes not to render the invisible visible and fixed but to trace the outlines of the apparition, summon the ghosts of those ignored, neglected, or oppressed. In conjuring them, he seeks their influence on the systems in which they live, whether those systems recognize them or not.

In one poem, Hayes repeats the N-word several times. The shock of it felt like a perfect combination of the volta and this conjuring—a moment in the reading that felt so different from the other pieces he read and the way he responded to so many questions. During the comments in the afternoon, he returned to that poem and told us he rarely uses the N-word. "That word," he called it. And, after he explained his word choice, it became an ever clearer moment of the poet striving *to poet*, to speak in a voice not his own to bring that other speaker back into the conversation. The N-word signals the turn and the ghost that returns, it history and effect made transparent rather than visible or invisible in this political moment.

Near the end of the conversation, one moderator asked Hayes, "Do you see the poet as the voice of dissent?" Hayes nodded. But, his body language more acknowledged the question, more than answered it in the affirmative. Earlier in the morning, when someone in the audience asked about the role of the poet in these times, Hayes responded that the poet needs "to poet." The teacher needs to teach, the singer needs to sing, the builder needs to build, he said. We all need to do what we do to make politics palpable. There is no one way of doing it. Perhaps, then, in these times, the poet needs to keep asking this question about dissent, Hayes seemed to be saying.

Hayes also gave us one more bit of advice before the close of the day's events: the new Kendrick Lamar album is great, he said. *Damn.* is better than, *To Pimp a Butterfly*, in his opinion. He told us he had been listening to *Damn.* and some work by the Irish musician Kate Tempest lately. And when one audience member shared his enthusiasm for Lamar's album, Hayes responded excitedly, adding that we should give a serious listen to the songs "Lust" and "DNA." In those tracks, whether or not Kendrick Lamar realized it, we could hear the volta and the ghosts conjured by his poetry.

Homeless Veterans Create Community Together on Beacon Hill

by Will Sweger

The first homeless encampment I visited was in Iraq along a tributary of the Tigris River. My platoon was conducting a census of squatters living outside company housing for a nearby oil-processing facility.

The camps make for fertile recruiting grounds for people willing to perform a variety of tasks associated with insurgency. You could make quick cash digging a hole in a road for someone else to come along and slip a homemade bomb into.

The people, like the reeds hugging to the moisture of the embankment, were sun-soaked and dusty. An old woman, her face a patchwork of wrinkles and open sores, stood watching us work outside the mud shanties.

Years later, I found myself visiting another homeless encampment. This one is in Seattle and populated by veterans. Residents of the lot have experiences of the Korean War, the Vietnam War, the Gulf War and the War in Afghanistan, a conflict spanning back 16 years.

Located near the Veterans Affairs Medical Center on Beacon Hill, the camp is made up of about 10 vehicles—mostly old RVs. Meeting me was a man who introduced himself as Cali. Having served as a combat engineer in the army, Cali, now 45, is employed as a construction worker. He lives in a single-room RV that's been in the lot 11 years and can no longer move under its own power.

Deftly managing his vape pen in a hand with a lopped-off finger, Cali speaks with casual profanity in rolling bursts as the moment takes him. He moved to Seattle about a year ago and began living in the lot, sleeping in his car. Another occupant, who'd lived in the lot for eight years and recently moved to a larger camper, offered his previous trailer as lodging.

The proximity to the medical center certainly played a part in Cali's choice to stay. He's undergoing treatment for a chronic back condition. "I love the Pacific Northwest," he said, "I love the way the VA takes care of us, I love that fact that my doctor does house calls, at least to us homeless people. How do you bitch about that?"

Yet living in an RV without power or plumbing presents unique challenges as well. "Being homeless is expensive," he said, explaining that without a refrigerator he is forced to buy groceries every day.

Mostly, he worries about a run in with parking enforcement. He says if he's at the trailer, the officers will usually avoid issuing him a citation. However, while he's at work, he worries he'll come home to find a ticket.

To get around needing a mailing address for his vehicle registration, he says several non-profits around town will receive mail for homeless people. However, he is unable to afford the fee for the new tabs that would get him out of paying for tickets. Additionally the camper portion of his trailer adds $350 to the vehicle registration cost and he can't afford to buy tabs at $550.

He also said he struggles every day to find a place to go to the bathroom and shower. Impressively, he casually recited the open hours of every building nearby with an available toilet.

Residents of the lot have a strict policy of never using VA trashcans for fear of reprisals. Most use bottles to relieve themselves, then take them to dumpsters elsewhere. "We get caught doing any of that, that's a fucking felony," Cali explained. "You're essentially dumping human waste, sewage, a biohazard in a trashcan. So we're running a risk just to take a shit every day."

Responding to the hostile environment, the residents of the lot have banned together in a sort of makeshift community, something that comes natural to many with the experience of wearing a uniform. In a way, the encampment becomes a patrol base and the residents become a unit.

Cali described veterans sweeping up parking stalls, likening their care to the military practice of a 'police call'—essentially walking together in a line over a site to make sure it is free of garbage and personal items. "It's a community," Cali said.

At one point, when the lock on the door of his RV broke, he felt comfortable going to work as other residents would keep an eye on his trailer for him.

The group will even host cookouts occasionally, typically drawing seven or eight attendees.

The VA Puget Sound Medical Care Public Affairs Office declined to comment on the lot near the hospital, citing that the land it sits on belongs to the city, not the medical facility. The King County Sherriff's office referred me to the Seattle Police Department. SPD failed to respond to my queries by publication time.

The encampment is unique in its cleanliness and its highly visible location, but ordinary in the precarious position it occupies straddling multiple agencies' jurisdictions. King County's count of people living without shelter increased this year to 11,643 individuals experiencing homelessness. Of that number, 2,314 are living in vehicles (about 1 in every 5 individuals without shelter).

Rebecca Murch, a U.S. Navy Veteran and Executive Director of Seattle Stand Down, a homeless veterans advocacy non-profit, met with me to discuss homeless veterans in Seattle. Referencing people sleeping in vehicles she explained "…more than likely they're probably parking illegally, they're being ticketed for various things, so now, as a society we've kind of criminalized homelessness. Now they have legal issues and financial issues…on top of the housing issues they already have."

Seattle City Council member Mike O'Brien has attempted to deal with the problem by proposing legislation to provide a path to amnesty for people living in their vehicles in the city. Scott Lindsay, formerly of Ed Murray's office, leaked the proposal, leading to critiques of allowing vehicles parking citation exemptions.

Interim mayor Tim Burgess recently announced increased funding in the city's budget for homeless services, but so far his office has not made a ruling about people living in vehicles. Until an official policy is adopted towards some sort of amnesty program, those living in vehicles will continue to camp on a precarious ledge.

In an interview, Council member O'Brien said, "We really do not have strategy around people living in vehicles." He is calling for the use of outreach teams dedicated to the unique needs of people coping with homelessness in vehicles. Current outreach centers are not set up to accommodate vehicle owners who would prefer the relative comfort and privacy of an RV to a crowded shelter.

"We were not getting the type of attention from the administration we wanted, so we started drafting the legislation," he said, pointing out the items addressed in the legislation could be implemented immediately through a mayor's executive order.

O'Brien added, "We've always recognized the point of the legislation was more about elevating the topic and getting some commitment to actually take some actions and ultimately build a strategy."

Citing the city's attempt at a managed safe lot in Ballard, O'Brien called it "an extremely expensive model" and went on to say, "If we're going to find solution that's financially sustainable, it's going to be incumbent upon the individuals to do a fair amount of self-management."

From safe lot locations, residents of vehicles could have access city resources aimed at helping them attain more-permanent housing, O'Brien said. In the model, city aid workers would be in encampments for a few hours a week rather than 24 hours a day, leading to lower costs for the city.

"Again, it's not going to work for everyone," he said, "I know there are some individuals who I've interacted with in vehicles who have a unique set of challenges…some of these folks may not work well in a self-managed encampment, it would be chaotic. For those folks we're going to need special resources."

He recognized city sweeps—where police and aid workers are involved for a short, but intense, period before the vehicles are moved to another part of the city—is very expensive and doesn't produce long-term housing outcomes.

"We have thousands of people on wait-lists trying to get into affordable housing spots," he said. "The reality is we're going to have thousands of people without housing until we can build a lot more affordable housing."

Talking with Cali, you get the sense the encampment is under siege. Even something as innocuous as a farmer's market may mean someone filing a report to the authorities. The veterans share the lot with an unofficial market every Friday and Saturday. Without portable toilets in the area, people relieve themselves on the side of trailers, something the vehicle residents fear may lead to reprisals due to complaints from VA employees using the lot during the day.

Their tenuous status sometimes creates stressful situations leading to threats of violence. Farmers' market vendors will arrive at between 1-2 a.m. Friday mornings. Hearing a loud conversation outside his window in the morning, Cali says he's emerged with a machete in one hand and a buck knife in the other to tell them to leave on more than one occasion. Most residents of the lot keep other weapons in their vehicles as well.

The veterans' camp seems excluded from most of the sweeps conducted in the city. Part of that might be the city's hesitance to forcibly remove veterans from their place near the VA hospital. The veterans themselves, sandwiched between a farmer's market, a hospital parking lot and a busy road are living on the edge.

Yet, surveying the lot, I saw gear neatly tucked under vehicles and a bird feeder hanging from one of the RVs. As Cali showed me the encampment, from the way he spoke about it I realized we were talking about his home. It was a reminder that individuals, wherever they find themselves, will try to find ways to make it comfortable and familiar.

People experiencing homelessness, whether they are in within sight of a golf course in Seattle or on the banks of the Tigris share a very human need for a safe, clean place to live. "We all got problems," Cali said, "I wish people would understand that just because I'm a veteran and just because I'm a disabled veteran, doesn't mean I'm broke."

"The Beachboyz" and Coach Corey Sampson Are the Real Deal

by Peter Johnson

Coach Corey Sampson's office is surprisingly comfortable. Its windowed door faces the Rainier Beach High School locker room. The coach's office is nearly as big as the team's, and the coach's office has its own bathroom. But, of course, it's a football office. And in football, authority is worshipped.

Sampson is not the curmudgeonly, grumpy man of few words that you would expect to coach the best South End team in a generation. He's animated, excited, and talks a mile a minute. He seems ready to jump out of his seat at any moment.

The coach is incredibly proud. Tonight is the last practice of the year. Tomorrow, the Rainier Beach Vikings play for the state championship.

For Sampson, it's vindication. He's the first black coach to take a team to the state football championship. Unlike the coaches at the area's football powerhouses—Eastside Catholic, Bellevue, O'Dea—Sampson doesn't have a full-time job coaching and teaching.

Sampson has been perpetually underestimated. He's been let go from two coaching jobs. His team has faced the same sort of condescension.

"We're overlooked a lot," Sampson says. "A lot of people think, the Rainier Beach area—they see there's a shooting, there's a drive-by, there's gang violence. They don't talk about the positives. You never hear about us giving clothes drives, us feeding the homeless."

It's a point of pride for Sampson that his program has achieved true excellence. The Vikings faced harder odds than most football powers to get to the state game. They weren't ranked. They even faced skepticism inside their own building.

"When I got here, I told the team trainer we were going to the playoffs that year," Sampson says. "She said, 'Ha ha, good luck.'"

She was right—sort of. They missed the playoffs by one game, going 6-3. But they've made the playoffs each of the three years since then. The Rainier Beach football team became the Beachboyz, a nickname that Sampson has emblazoned on stickers and t-shirts.

It was a lot of work. Clearly, Sampson is a talented football coach. But it's what he does outside the big office and cramped locker room that makes him special.

"Kids know what I want," Sampson says. "I built a relationship with the teachers, and walked around the hallways. I'd say, 'Get out the hallways. Get off your cell phone. Go to class. Don't skip class.' So then they knew what I was about."

Some of Sampson's team still cuts class and acts out—teenagers will be teenagers, after all—but he says that his team's behavior in school has improved. He finds out about it right away, and acts fast to hold his students accountable.

"It's building that tough love," Sampson says. "That hard discipline. I let those guys know that's our expectation. Discipline, being accountable. Just as hard as you try on the football field, try as hard in the classroom. Don't do nothing that you wouldn't do in front of your mom—always think that eyes are watching you. This is what we need to do to be successful in life."

Sampson leads by example. He's been on campus every day (except Sundays) since March, leading practices, meeting with teachers, and getting to know his students better. Sampson fundraises relentlessly—the Vikings have six uniform designs and two helmets, compared to one incomplete set when he started—and he's been able to raise money to take the team on a retreat and to out-of-state road games.

Sampson and one of his assistants also feed the entire team dinner on Thursday and Friday. That's partly for team-building, but it's also prosaic.

"Some kids don't have food. Some of 'em don't have anywhere to eat. They're hungry."

Sampson has created a close-knit team culture. The kids are loose and animated when I walk into the locker room. A big, junior year offensive lineman is sitting on top of the lockers, singing and rapping. A very small freshman receiver is getting him to crack up as they pull on their pads and cleats.

When we go out to the field to watch the team's walk-throughs—Sampson runs a college-style spread offense with sophisticated zone blocking, a scheme that's more advanced than most high school offenses—Sampson checks in with the players he sees. One is lagging in the locker room, and Sampson makes sure he's feeling right. Other players come up and ask questions. It's clear that they trust him.

"I was one of these kids, so I know," Sampson says. "I can relate to 'em. I didn't have a father. As I got older, my coaches helped mentor me, so coaching and giving back to the community, and helping mentor these kids—I talk to em, I love em, I hug em. And I give some of them second chances. Some of them do deserve second chances."

Sampson is clear-eyed about the structural barriers his team faces. Mass incarceration has taken its toll on the majority-black team. "I got 30 something, 40 something kids, and only three have their dads."

Race has spilled over to the field. Last year, the Vikings lost to Bellingham football powerhouse Squalicum in the second round of the playoffs. The game ended in a loss with four minutes left on the clock. Squalicum's provocations and chippy play caused the Vikings' tempers to snap. A fight broke out. Sampson says that racist behavior by Squalicum instigated the fight.

"They were pulling our face masks off, ripping off our helmets, throwing punches on the ground, calling us names," Sampson says. "I tried to tell the ref to control the game, but he told *me* to shut up and told our kids to be quiet."

He says that the team was portrayed as thugs in subsequent press coverage of the game.

"They made us out to be this big, bad villain. We're not wild dogs, animals. That hurt me. That really, really hurt me."

Sampson used the game and the dust-up as a teaching moment. He wants to make sure his kids get to use their scholarships—seven Vikings have Division 1 football offers this year, and all but one PAC 12 school visited practice—instead of getting stuck in the school to prison pipeline.

"What they did to us in the game, it's messed up," Sampson says. "But I told the guys, that's how life is. You gotta watch how you move around, because they're automatically thinking that you're an animal outta control. If you do anything wrong, it's gonna be magnified."

"That's something they got to deal with in society. Do you react to it, or do you think about it? I'm always telling guys, you need to think about it before you react, and just walk away from it. If you just react, and you do something that you don't want to happen, you're gonna wind up someplace you don't wanna be at, or locked up."

The air was crisp and cold. Out on the field, as the punt unit was practicing, the other thirty boys ran drills, joked, and talked trash to each other. A bad snap dribbled past the punter, and one of Sampson's assistants got right on the center. Sampson, who was nearly manic during our interview, watched it play out calmly, and went over to give the line some advice.

Sampson strode back to the sideline and slowed his pace. All his work, and his teams', was coming to fruition. He was savoring the moment, even though he'd had to put on long johns and an extra set of warm up pants to ward off the early winter cold. He was smiling.

"Man," he said, "I love November football."

To All Good Men: You Must be Braver

by Danica Bornstein

Reading all the recent accounts of sexual harassment and assault, I've been remembering what it was like to experience sexism as a very, very young woman.

I still experience sexism of course, but now it's more in the form of a male colleague who looks surprised every time I say something smart, even though I've literally said something smart every time we've ever talked, or the helpful gentlemen of the internet who make themselves available to explain things about which I'm already quite knowledgeable, such as my own experiences, or fundamental and obvious facts of human life.

When I was a very young woman the way sexism landed on me was different. It was mostly a constant onslaught of invasions and threats to my physical, sexualized body. So many of us experience harassment and violence during these early years. The world is very unfair to young women in that their bodies are seen as objects to exploit and grab, at just the developmental moment when we are most vulnerable to being intimidated, manipulated, overwhelmed, and disbelieved because we are still relatively new at life. It's extremely ugly, exploitative, and cruel.

I wasn't an actor or an "important" person so I didn't know a Harvey Weinstein, but I had the men around me to deal with. I worked at a café. Some of the men who worked there were chill and just doing their jobs, some were very gentle, and some were actual friends who talked with me about things like music, and books, and my life.

But there was also the one I barely knew because of our opposite shifts who pinned me against a stack of boxes in the walk-in, knocking the wind out of me while kissing me and touching my body. There was the one who would watch me while I worked; if I bent down I might stand up to find him frozen mid-action, openly gaping at my breasts or ass. And the one who would grab my arm if he could catch me and, pinning my wrist, spread chocolate on my skin and try to lick it off.

I remember that, when I had to walk to the back of the café, I would gear up to be quick and agile and ready to fight, but not fight too hard, because its work and these are coworkers. Bear in mind that at this point I was a 15 or 16-year-old person, earning $2 an hour plus tips, trying to perform the functions of my job, setting dirty dishes in a tub or getting berries to garnish a plate.

It never once occurred to me to tell the owners. My manager, a woman, certainly knew but I believe that, like me, she saw these experiences as merely one of the facts of a woman's life.

I also remember all the work that went into making sure I was seen as an attractive, but not slutty, person. To be seen as unattractive was to risk becoming irrelevant and giving up the little power and influence I seemed to have. But to be seen as a slut seemed dangerous beyond measure.

Even as a white girl and a high-achieving student—the kind of girl who is seen as relatively valuable and deserving of respect—I was subject to a tremendous amount of violence. I did not feel I could afford to do one single thing that might cause me to be held in less regard.

This is an important aspect of white privilege, and it's a common conversation amongst white people: whether or not it is true that white people in poverty or experiencing violence and adversity are still benefiting from white privilege. Of course we are. Whiteness serves as an invisible shield that, even under egregious conditions, is protecting us in ways we can't see. Even a terrible situation can always be much, much worse.

I didn't necessarily understand this in terms of whiteness at that time but I understood that I was seen as a somewhat worthy but exploitable person, and I didn't have one ounce of worthiness that I could afford to lose. My G-d, if this is how "good" girls are treated—if I'm seen as bad or dirty, I will surely die.

When I meet women who have found a way to explore their sexuality openly and to embrace a kind of "sluttiness", I feel happy for them. I also feel profound envy of their ability to behave as free persons and I feel profound grief. I don't know if I would have enjoyed being a sluttier person but I would have liked the safety and the space to find out.

Rape culture has many, many unseen costs, and this is one of them: it makes us police ourselves before we can even know who we are. I wanted to live, and the only way I knew to do that was to limit myself and be the safest kind of girl that was possible for me.

I woke up the other day thinking about nice guys and good men, and how much, and how little, we expect and receive from them. I thought about the men I worked with at the café who were friends and good people, and about what they did and did not do. They listened to me and treated me as an interesting person with ideas, which I was. I had already experienced a lot of sexual violation by older men, and I cherished safe, non-sexual attention from adult men; they offered this very generously. They lent me books and traded tapes with me.

I confided in one of these coworkers when I was sexually assaulted by a relative. I was 16 and he was 24. I was telling him what happened and it sounded so absurd and unthinkable that I said, "Wait. This doesn't sound true. I might be making it up." He told me fiercely, "No! Don't ever think that. That's what they want you to think. You're telling the truth. You did not make it up." I have held that moment in my heart for 30 years.

But what he did not do—what none of the good men at the cafe ever did—was turn to their coworkers and tell them to stop. They didn't tell the other men to stop touching me or grabbing me or watching my body when I moved. They supported me as a person, and they were good to me, but they were not willing to have conflict with other men.

What I want the men in my life to know is that its not possible to have it both ways: you can't have womxn's backs without standing up to other men. Please let go of that dream. It isn't possible. In the wake of many "me too" conversations, many men are asking what they can do. Speaking for myself, this is what I want: I want the men who care for me to be braver in their relationships with other men. The niceness, the unwillingness to ruffle feathers or have awkward conversations—it's literally killing us.

I know that talking with other men about the humanity of womxn is a difficult and sometimes frightening task and I know this in two ways.

First, I have been doing it my entire life without much help from good men and I know that, when challenged on their oppressive behavior, men can be punitive, dismissive, violent, and cruel. Men don't want to be on the receiving end of this, but honestly, neither do we.

I also know it's a difficult task because, as a white person, I have found talking with other white people about racism and white supremacy is not very pleasant either. When challenged on micro-aggressions, or not-so-micro-aggressions, white folks can get defensive, cry, threaten, and make excuses. It's uncomfortable; it does not feel good.

But if I'm going to have any accountability at all to the people of color who I love and who are part of my community, I have to fight my way through these conversations. I'm not in any way bragging about my work in this area. I fail more than I succeed, and I'm very often disappointed in myself. But if I'm not challenging myself to have these hard conversations with other white folks then the love I have for the people of color in my life lacks integrity and rigor, and I'm not worthy of their trust.

The same is true for men. If you love and support us, but you're not willing to have uncomfortable conversations with other men in support of our humanity, that love is thin and incomplete. Love without action is just sentiment, lacking teeth and claws, and truly, it is not something I can trust or rely on. I don't mean to be harsh; I'm only asking of you what I am asking of myself. You'll fail just like I fail, but if your love does not have a dimension of rigor and risk, if your love is not fighting for me, then what is it?

I have been thinking so much lately about hearing each other and seeing each other, showing up for each other, and taking risks for each other. The bittersweet thing is that we need each other so much as accomplices, collaborators, and allies, yet its always true that by the time we show up to do that, we are late. Not too late, necessarily, but late.

I feel this when I read men's heartfelt responses to #MeToo. I think, "I need you so much and I'm so glad you are here," and I also think, "I've been saying this for years. Where have you been?!" I'm hopeful, and the pain and anger are also very deep.

The same is true for many of us non-black folks in our response to state violence against black bodies. It took the advent of bodycams and the internet for us to believe that what black people have been reporting for centuries —centuries!—was the truth. It is shameful and it is late. And it is also the most I have seen in my lifetime of us showing up for each other, and I want it to grow.

In this hardest time, when the earth is burning and drowning, when our greatest cruelties against each other are being exposed, I am daring to hope that we are learning how to listen to and believe and take risks for each other.

We need each other. We are all we have.

The Indispensable History and Counter-narrative The Journal of Ben Uchida: Citizen 13559 Taught My Son

by Sharon H Chang

"How many of you have experienced racism, bullying, or teasing? Raise your hand." The actors ask the audience to close our eyes so answers will be confidential, but I feel my son lift his hand beside me. My heart is pained, suddenly awash in blues, purples, and greys. Later I ask my son—has he experienced all three things? Bullying, teasing, and racism? He nods his head assuredly, says yes, "All of it."

This weekend I took my 8-year-old Japanese Mixed American son to his first play *The Journal of Ben Uchida: Citizen 13559* at the Seattle Children's Theater (SGT). The historical play, adapted by Naomi Iizuka from Barry Denenberg's 2003 novel of the same name, follows the internment of a Japanese American family during World War II as seen through the eyes and journaling of the family's youngest member, Ben Uchida.

Ben Uchida (played by Mikko Juan) is an enthusiastic 12-year-old boy who adores his hardworking optometrist father Masao Uchida (played by Ray Tagavilla). Mr. Uchida has dutifully bought into the sanguine immigrant stereotype–that if you pull yourself up by your bootstraps and don't rock the boat, anyone can achieve the American Dream. It's a patriotic lesson he imparts optimistically to his son and family as, certainly, it has seemed to work for him. But the father's core beliefs are put to the test when Pearl Harbor is bombed and the entire family is suddenly rounded up, sent to prison camp in the desert, and loses everything but each other.

The Uchidas are fictional but their story is based on the real stories of thousands of Japanese Americans forced into U.S. prison camps in the mid-twentieth century. Following the Japanese attack on Pearl Harbor, President Franklin D. Roosevelt signed Executive Order 9066 on February 19, 1942, which paved the way for the racist incarceration of more than 110,000 Japanese Americans until the end of the war. Multiracial Japanese Americans, like my son and husband, were also sent to live in the camps even if they had as little as "1/16" Japanese heritage.

Each member of the Uchida family processes this trauma with complex human difference. Mr. Uchida sinks into a deep depression. Ben becomes buried in his thoughts and journals ferociously. By contrast, his teenage sister Naomi (played by Mi Kang) becomes angry and defiant, demanding answers to hard questions, like, "Why are we being sent away!?" Meanwhile, their good-natured mother Mrs. Uchida (played by Annie Yim) grabs a broom and obsessively tries to control the dust, lint, and dirt in their barracks even though it just keeps reappearing the next day.

There are tough encounters with various white characters (played by Brenda Joyner and Conner Nedderson) some of which can be very hard to watch. "Jap!" "Slant-eyed Chink!" "The only good Jap is a dead Jap!" Lines like these were excruciating for me to hear as a person of Taiwanese/Chinese descent. It was even harder, however, to see my wide-eyed Japanese/Taiwanese/Chinese child hear the same, realizing those words were meant for him too. At one point my son even sucked in his breath when white characters appeared onstage, whispering anxiously to me, "Here comes more white people."

Seattle Children's Theatre recommends 9+ for heavy content such as this: racism, slurs, profiling, aggression, violence, and suicide. But I think many parents of color realize our children don't have the luxury of waiting to talk about and process these things. My son at eight years old—as he is well aware–has already experienced racism. He was mislabeled an English Language Learner by Seattle Public Schools beginning in kindergarten; endured other students saying his Japanese name wrong all of first grade with no support from his white teacher; is being called "Chinese boy" in second grade by his peers and sees daily how children like him are rarely represented, or represented as stereotypes, in the books he reads, shows and movies he watches, and video games he plays.

To the point, People of Color need our histories to help us understand and contextualize the way we're treated in this majority-white nation practically from the time we're born. Yet what is taught to us in school persists in being mostly white-washed, invisibilizing the stories of our predecessors which keeps us disoriented and silent. So, I have complete clarity around the fact that I am the one who needs to make sure this education happens for my child. Meaning that even though my son did not meet SCT's age recommendation, I took him to see *The Journal of Ben Uchida* anyway.

And I'm so glad I did.

Knowing accurate histories helps People of Color know where we stand, gives us the tools to navigate a highly racialized society and fight to be heard. It also helps us show up for the struggles of others. True, the play was heavy. I cried often and know my son felt emotional too. But afterward, the questions my son has been asking and the connections he keeps making are truly inspiring.

For instance, my son wondered if the performers knew the picture book *Baseball Saved Us*, by Ken Mochizuki. I was surprised and impressed he remembered this book about an interned Japanese American community finding resilience in creating their own camp baseball league. We hadn't read the book in a long time but he recalled it right away, clearly noting the similarities (which shows how important it is for us to read books to our children of color that reflect the experiences of people like them).

Following, we acknowledged the Japanese American people we know today, our friends and neighbors, who have family members that were interned. My son also wanted to know a lot more about his own Japanese immigrant grandmother, his Obaachan; about when and where she was born, her relationship to the war, as well as her immigration story.

For these reasons, and so many more, I can't recommend this play enough. Especially for Asian American families.

The Journal of Ben Uchida runs a little over an hour with a short talkback at the end, well-facilitated by the actors, which you should stay for. Additionally, SGT has produced a meticulous, in-depth audience guide available online. The guide is an incredible resource comprising detailed descriptions of costume and set design, a conversation with Director Desdemona Chiang, and important historical context on the forced removal of Japanese Americans from Western Washington.

You know, when my son was a preschooler he went through a phase where he was obsessed with depictions of blond-haired, blue-eyed white boys. He would stare at said images, let me know out loud that he liked them best, and sometimes, when asked about his own appearance would even say he looked like those white boys (which he doesn't). It was horrible, and we have worked together for years to try to undo this internalized oppression and help him celebrate instead who he really is.

After years of counter-narrating at home, I can't say this sense of racial inferiority in him has been fully erased. But I can say that my son has learned to appreciate and seek out, with pride, depictions of children and people who look like him. And I know this is true because upon seeing *The Journal of Ben Uchida*—though Japanese American characters were oppressed, put down, had everything taken away from them—now it wasn't the light-haired white characters my son wanted to be.

He said, he liked Ben Uchida best.

An Open Letter to Persons with Guns, Especially Persons under 25

by Georgia S. McDade

Before you shoot and kill someone accidentally or intentionally, know that your life will be forever divided into Before the Shooting (BTS) and After the Shooting (ATS). Regardless of what ails you now and how bad you think life is, life will be worse ATS. If you think you were bored before, consider being confined to an 8ft by 6ft cell indefinitely. Although you may be released early, you may remain much longer than decreed.

If you peruse all the activities listed in the Thursday and Friday newspapers and see "nothing to do," imagine—you probably can't—not knowing how long you will be confined 23 of 24 hours, 7 of 7 days doing what someone tells you to do.

Think what your confinement does to your mom, dad, siblings, grandparents, aunts and uncles, friends, anyone who cares about you. How often can they visit? What do they have to do to get to you? Is there a car? Is the car in good shape? Must your mom, sister, aunt, wife or girlfriend—female visitors outnumber the male visitors by a large number—get someone to bring her at that person's convenience? Is there money to pay that person? Did you ever visit a prison? Do you know what visitors endure before they can see you?

Granted, some officials are kinder, more respectful than others, but treatment of the visitor depends on the person in charge. At any time, a visitor may be taken to another space to be patted down. Believe me: this can be embarrassing, humiliating. With so much on their minds, visitors do not always remember to wear certain shoes, clothes, lingerie.

Prepare to accept a culture new to you. Persons you might never have met—never wanted to meet—you now encounter. Respect? Understanding? Concern? Who cares about your needs? For the most part, forget your wants. Learn to be on guard—your waking and sleeping hours. Count on yourself for protection. Stay healthy—there is no guarantee you will get health care, adequate health care. If you are blessed to have someone send you something—know there is no guarantee of getting it. There's a long list of what you may or may not receive. Your mail is read and may be returned to the sender if it violates the code.

Everything you were accustomed to for holidays—your family or a houseful of folks or just your boys—has ended, at least for now. Forget celebrating birthdays, checking cellphones. If you can afford the cheap cable, you may get to watch some of your favorite television programs or see new movies as they come to television. Forget dining at your favorite restaurants, any restaurants. No more going to church on special occasions if only to please your mom or grandmother.

Nieces and nephews may forget you; others won't meet you until they are too old to be thrown in the air or ride on your shoulders or back. You'll miss all kinds of events that cannot be repeated. If a loved one—mom and dad, sister and brother included—is sick or dies, there's a chance you will not be allowed to visit or attend the service. If you are permitted to go, you will have very limited time before returning to prison.

If you are released—3479 persons died in prisons in 2013—you have another battle on your hands. Know now that "freedom" does not mean you are free; it means you are no longer behind physical bars. You will forever lack the freedom of those who did not go to prison. Where will you stay? If you do not have family willing to take you in, you must go to a group home, find a room, or apartment. Getting an apartment won't be easy. Landlords ask, "Are you a felon?" Some landlords stop when they get a yes answer; others say, "Did you assault or murder anyone?" A yes most likely means a no for that place. Some states won't let you get Section 8 housing, probably all you can afford with the Social Security benefits you may collect.

The few hundred dollars you may have accumulated while in prison does not go very far. Some states demand restitution which may be thousands of dollars, and garnishment is not uncommon. If you managed to get a GED, an associate, a bachelor's, a master's while confined, your education will not give you the boost it usually gives a graduate. Finding a job won't be easy. No experience, no work history creates problems. Some states will not let you vote—ever. If you do not have a job or only a minimum-wage job because you have no training or experience, you do not have much money.

Because justice so often sits, stands, lies beyond so many in our society, especially persons whose skin has a certain degree of melanin and persons who have little or no money, persons who have little or no education, you should make not entering the "justice' system your goal. One instant can change your life, the lives of those you love, the lives of persons you do not know. Be careful. Many innocent persons are incarcerated. Many persons who are guilty do not deserve the sentences they receive. So, if you commit a serious crime, one with a gun, you are putting yourself on a negative course that you may never be able to make positive.

Just think about this.

A COMMUNITY SPIRIT THAT IS BULLET PROOF

by Miguel Jimenez

There were ten shots fired. Or at least that's what I think we counted while sitting at a large table near the front window of Rainier Beach's Jude's Old Town last Tuesday.

Darting to the back of the bar, all of us crouched to survey the scene from the large front windows. The disparate conversations broke apart as the whole bar began asking questions and assembling facts. There was a palpable sense of caution bordering on fear, but certainly not panic.

I called the last member of my friend group who was still on his way to make sure he was ok. I don't want to normalize the incident, as if this is a regular occurrence that happens all the time in South Seattle, and I cringe at the thought of the next Seattle Times article about the story.

After a few more minutes of silence we walked back to our conversation at the table by the window, yet my mind was elsewhere. I kept thinking about the shooter. No one deserves to live in a place that is unsafe, where they fear for their life. This feels especially true for that individual. What drove this person to a place where they made the decision to open fire out of the window of a moving vehicle on a busy Rainier Avenue at 6:00pm in the evening? I thought about the reactions reporters would be trying to get after the story.

"Where were you and how did you feel?"

I thought about who I would have chosen to interview. Maybe I would have called up Marvin Charles from the D.A.D.S program. Marvin and his wife Jeanett, along with their team, have been working at South Lake High School to help young fathers remain a constant presence in their children's lives.

They are part of a system of organizations trying to ensure teens act responsibly by leading with example. Or maybe I would try to find a minute with Dominique Davis who runs Community Passageways. His organization works with youth who have already entered the judicial system.

They work to help youth process trauma while beginning to deal with this country's astronomical rates of recidivism.

The shooting stirred up a lot emotion for me and my neighbors and colleagues around the table. We each shared our experiences, and lack thereof, surrounding shootings during our lifetime. We were frustrated and exasperated, but not for a minute did I ever think "I need to leave this bar" or "I need to move out of this neighborhood" or even "I need to leave this city".

For us life continues. Our meeting continued. We continued to discuss our plans to build a youth employment training program. The work continues.

ACKNOWLEDGEMENTS

꙳

Marcus Harrison Green would like to first thank the entire South Seattle community for their continued support of the *South Seattle Emerald*.

An immense thank you to Vlad Verano for his tremendous patience, creativity, and time in engineering all our anthologies to date!

Much appreciation to the *South Seattle Emerald* board, past and present, including Devin Chicras, Bridgette Hempstead, Seferiana Day, Dominic Smargiassi, Andrew Johnston, Nick Patterson, Dustin Washington, Ijeoma Oluo, Alan Preston, Jovelle Tamayo, Emanuel da Silva, Maia Segura, Marissa Tsaniff, and Dominique Scalia.

Thank you to Marilee Jolin for going above and beyond the call of duty as the *Emerald*'s first Executive Director, and an equal thank you to Regent Brown who is currently fulfilling that role.

To my parents Phillip and Cynthia Green, theirs is no higher honor than being called your son. Thank you both for your sustained belief in and past sacrifices for my dreams.

And last, but certainly far from least, a full-hearted thank you to every single contributor in this book!

About the Editor

Marcus Harrison Green, is the co-founder of the *South Seattle Emerald*, a former Reporting Fellow with *YES!* Magazine, a board member of the Western Washington Chapter of the Society of Professional Journalists and a recipient of Cross Cut's Courage Award for Culture.

Growing up in South Seattle, he experienced first-hand the neglect of news coverage in the area by local media, which taught him the value of narratives.

After an unfulfilling stint working for a Los Angeles based hedge-fund in his twenties, Marcus returned to his community determined to tell its true story, which led him to start the *South Seattle Emerald*.

The publication has become a go-to source of community information in a part of the city that rarely receives much press outside of the police blotter. As he says "The media spends so much time talking about the death here, that it rarely ever talks about the abundance of life also found here."

Green sees storytelling, particularly journalism as democracy's most essential tool. He says its function is not only to speak truth to power, since the powerful most often already knows the truth, which is usually why they try to hide it.

Journalism's true job, he says, is to speak truth to the many who believe they are powerless; it reminds them they aren't.

He is proud to live in the "South End" of Seattle.

CPSIA information can be obtained
at www.ICGtesting.com
Printed in the USA
FSHW01n2244200618
49646FS

9 781609 441326